I0182562

Mastering Girlhood To Womanhood

BOOK 5

LESSONS 22-24

MASTERING GIRLHOOD TO WOMANHOOD
BOOK 5
LESSONS 22-24

Juanita B. Tischendorf

Copyright Page

THIS IS A J. TISCHENDORF BOOK
PUBLISHED BY J TISCHENDORF SERVICES

Copyright © 2018 by Juanita B. Tischendorf

All rights reserved. Published in the United States by J. Tischendorf
Services

www.lulu.com

Library of Congress Cataloging in-Publication Data
Tischendorf, Juanita, [date]
MASTERING GIRLHOOD TO WOMANHOOD LESSONS 22-24 /
Juanita Tischendorf – 1st ed.
p.   cm.

Step by Step Instructional manual for teen girls

No part of this publication may be reproduced, stored in a retrieval
system or transmitted in any way by any means, electronic, mechanical,
photocopy, recording or otherwise without the prior permission of the
author except as provided by USA copyright law.

Book design copyright © 2018 by J Tischendorf Services. All rights
reserved.

Published in the United States of America

ISBN: 978-1-928613-43-5 (Hardcover)
ISBN: 978-1-928613-42-8 (Paperback)
ISBN: 978-1-928613-89-3 (E-Book)

Dedication

This book is dedicated to those teenage girls who want to be the best they can be. Mastering Girlhood To Womanhood is a class of instructions that has equal doses of euphoria and agony, and like every part of life, it takes willpower along with dedication to face the journey.

This is the beginning of a four-book presentation of working toward all the aspects that make you who you are. Each book covers a segment of your development until you reach the end. At that point you will know yourself better than you ever thought possible. From your outward appearance, your inward feelings, and your ability to make it in this world.

If this is what you hope for, these books will get you there.

Epigraph

"Stanford Encyclopedia of Philosophy"

The nature of beauty is one of the most enduring
and controversial themes in Western philosophy, and is—
with the nature of art—one of the two fundamental issues
in philosophical aesthetics. Beauty has traditionally been
counted among the ultimate values, with goodness, truth,
and justice.

Preface

Have you ever felt pulled or twisted from the path you had chosen; as if forces beyond control were at the wheel and you were merely a passenger? If not, you are a lucky person and if so, don't think for a minute you are the only one who has felt as though the oars were being wield by others.

It appears all the important parts of life are controlled and we are merely pawns playing a role. One attempt to make sense of it all is to think that no matter how determined you are to follow the callings of your heart or aim to force yourself to do what is right, it is not your choice that guides you to the outcome. No, it is something called 'destiny' that sits in the driver's seat.

The story I am about to tell you will make a believer out of you or at least have you wondering if it could have been. Because one thing is sure, destiny can lead you into situations that are not as they seem to be.

CONTENTS

INTRODUCTION

Believe it or not, you have reached the end of your journey in learning all there is to learn about you. You should be glowing with confidence and now how and you have a right to. Now, this last book will challenge what you have learned in that it is applying your training to entering the work force. You can only grow more by going through these lessons.

LESSON 22:
WORLD OF MODELING

If you have started with the first lesson in this series, by the time you reach this section you have the "basics" of modeling. But there are other points that need to be covered that pertain to anyone entering the modeling field. By now the confidence in yourself has been built so that whatever avenue you want to choose, the door is open. You are a new person with feelings of your accomplishments helping it grow each day. You are ready.

I don't need to tell you that what you have learned is all a part of succeeding in modeling and I don't need to stress the importance of using all that you have learned each day as a part of your continual self-development. The aim now is to give you the additional information that will help you master the "art" of modeling.

If there is one field that can perfect all that you are, it's modeling. This is not an easy field to enter, but with the proper training and knowhow, you can succeed. All it takes is wanting this for yourself and being willing to work at knowing you are the best you can be. This and your confidence will help you overcome the obstacles that are bound to appear as you seek success in your chosen field.

Young people, and especially the beginning models seem to confuse prettiness with beauty. True beauty is the result of hard work, determination, and above all having the proper state of mind. Your attitude and state of mind will be the key to seeing your dream come true. Start learning not to pick at your faults or even ask yourself the question of your ability to become as beautiful as a model. You must be honest with yourself but not challenge yourself.

You must decide what it is that you want and then intelligently go after it and you must make an honest appraisal of yourself and learn what it is that you can improve on. Remember that beauty is an impression that is created by an attitude of being beautiful. You must think beautiful, dress beautiful and act beautiful and then, you will be beautiful.

There are few career choices more rewarding for an ambitious, attractive, and determined young woman than a career in modeling. All around the world modeling has become a symbol of status. For their contribution to advertising (television commercials, magazine print work, catalogs, fashion shows, etc.) models have become indispensable. Knowing what you need to know about modeling can be a starting point in entering a career as a manufacturers' representative or the business world, a career in fashion as stylists, and makeup artists. And for those who look toward staying in the limelight there is the hope of using your modeling background as a stepping stone for entering the star-studded field of the filming world. Not only will you find modeling a wonderful experience that can help you for the rest of your life, but through the experience you will gain poise, self-confidence and the ability to perfect your total look which will aid you in any career.

We all have heard of the many success stories of individuals who "make it". With each success story, there is a pattern. The pattern is simply knowing the right people, having knowledge of the opportunity, and most importantly, being at the right place at the right time!"

My responsibility to any client is simply to help them find the best of themselves, play upon it and bring it out in the open in a manner that reflects their personality. Once carried out, the next step is to encourage and assist them in the direction they wish to go. The following information should be seen as a vital part of your training.

Though not a part of "The Selfie" if you have worked through all the lessons of "The Selfie" what follows will be familiar to you. If you began with the first book in the self-development series (The Selfie book in sections) you are ready for this lesson.

I believe in you and will be your best fan.

On Being A Model

A good posture is an absolute necessity for modeling. Without good posture you cannot meet the criteria of gracefulness that every good model has. Look at the diagram. Perfect posture is like standing with a board extending down the back of you from your head to toe. You feel like a string runs from your feet up to your head, pulled upward forcing your body to extend its full length. It is important that you learn how to get into the proper standing position.

Proper walking begins with learning how to stand properly and then carrying that stance through as you step forward.

Poise & Posture

You may be saying to yourself at this moment, poise and posture are one and the same. Not so! Let's study the terms.

Poise is self-assurance of manner, a tact in coping graciously, and a way of carrying oneself.

Posture is a conscious mental behavioral attitude that is either a characteristic or assumed position of the body for a specific purpose. Think of it in terms of the pose of a model or an artistic figure. The difference in the two terms will become clearer as you work through this lesson.

How important are poise and posture? Well, have you ever thought a photograph of you didn't look like you at all? That's because even though the photograph has your features, it lacks your expression or how you visualize yourself to look. The way you move, stand, sit, use your hands, and place your feet are as much a part of your expression as your hair, eyes, mouth, or nose. To have a picture look like you, it must be a still shot of *YOU* in motion.

The same principle holds true when people meet you. If you stare at them in a motionless state, it's like viewing the photograph or mirror image of you. Not only is it your features, but the way you move and feel about yourself that tends to accentuate or obliterate the overall picture. That's where poise and posture come in.

You can be perfectly put together, but if your motion says something different, you've not gained a thing from the effort. To have people view you as refined you must know how to move so that you appear to glide down a flight of stairs, dance as you walk, or float into a chair. Every woman is more than a pretty head of hair, a good figure, or a wonderful complexion. Her confidence must also be reflected in her motions.

Remember as a child playing "*Freeze*"? You would be whirled around by another child, let go, and once released you were to *freeze* into position. The final frozen motion was always funny. Don't let yourself be judged by a motion that no longer fits the situation.

Poise, the movement of a truly confident woman is not achieved by accident. It is acquired through knowledge and hard work. A lot of it comes from inner confidence and confidence comes from knowing what to do.

Posture

The most essential part of beautiful coordination comes from correct posture and posture is the key to a more graceful you. To be poised, you must have perfect posture. Our first step then is to check your posture.

Stand as straight as you can in front of a full-length mirror and look very closely at the way you hold your head, the position of your shoulders, chest, stomach, hips, knees, and arms. Think about these areas of your body and try and describe to yourself how each part feels as you stand erect. Take a piece of paper and write down a description of the position of your body as you stood erect and look at your notes as you go over the following areas.

HEAD
Is your head erect, your chin parallel to the floor? Do you feel as if a string extends from the top of your head to the ceiling, pulling your head up?

SHOULDERS
Are your shoulders back and dropped in a relaxed position? Do you feel as though your neck is extending its full length?

CHEST
Is your chest held high? Do you feel as though your chest is lifting up and out?

WAIST
Are you stretched long through your waist? Do you feel as though you are standing taller?

STOMACH
Is your stomach held in. Do you feel as if a wide metal ring were squeezing around your waist?

BUTTOCKS
Are your buttocks tucked under by tipping the pelvic bone forward and up? If you can

feel weight settling down on your hips you are not tipping the pelvic bone.

JOINTS Are your knees relaxed, your elbows slightly bent, your wrists held so that palms turn in toward your body?

Stand in front of the mirror again and this time make sure that all areas of your body are in proper alignment. Hold the position and concentrate so that you can begin to feel the correct posture of your body.

Now stand with your back against a wall; heels two inches from the baseboard. Assume your perfect posture position: head erect, stretching long in waist, rolling pelvis forward and up, knees relaxed. Place your hand on your tummy and press your spine back on the wall. You should feel the pelvis lift.

Move a hand back and feel to see if there is any space between the small of your back and the wall. There should be no space. If there is, concentrate very hard on rotating your pelvis forward until the space disappears.

If you cannot press your back flat against the wall, try this trick. Slide your back down the wall until you are in a sitting position. This will bring your spine to the proper alignment. Then slowly slide back up the wall keeping your spine straight until you are once again standing up. Maintain this position.

Concentrate! You must feel it, sense the proper location of every part of your body and record the feeling of perfect posture in your mind so that you can put your body in place without having to look in a mirror or use a wall for judgment. This may feel awkward and unnatural at first, but don't worry it will begin to feel comfortable and instinctive with practice.

Since you can't always edge up to a wall as a posture test, you must carry the image of the wall and how it feels when you are standing properly. Once you have conquered the perfect posture position, you next need to learn how to walk properly.

Walking Proudly

When your body is a mass of disorganized bones and muscles, you are bound to tire when you walk. The upper part of your body settles down on your legs as if they were wooden stands and they will ache. Your feet feel the effect and protest at every step you take. The weight settling down crowds the spine into a crooked position and you soon have a back ache. All this discomfort can't help but show in your expression.

If this is what is happening when you find you must walk for extended periods or even short spurts, you are creating a negative impression of you. Walking with your head down gives a sense of sadness to your demeanor, slump shoulder's gives a feeling of dejection, and stride may project a bossy attitude. None of these are what you strive to portray so let's learn the art of walking proudly.

Move up against a wall and when you have your body in alignment, step away from the wall and maintain your perfect posture as you walk across the room. To do this properly, look over the following:

1) Start by lifting your thigh slightly and concentrate so you don't lead with your shoulders.

2) Move your thigh first.

3)   For women, the space between your steps should be no longer than the length of your foot, even shorter if you find it comfortable. Too long a stride is masculine, too short a stride looks prissy.

4)   On each step your heel should touch the floor first, then quickly shift the weight forward to the entire foot as you take the next step. It will be easier to get the right walking "feel" if you keep your feet close to the ground when you lift them.

5)   Your arms should hang relaxed at your sides, palms toward the thigh, barely touching them as they swing forward to the front of your body, ever so slightly. Your elbows should be in close to your waist. Remember, it's palms in, elbows close, and shoulders relaxed.

6)   As you walk keep your toes pointed straight ahead and place your feet directly to the side of an imaginary line running down the center. Do not step on this line. Your right foot should be on the right side of the line, left foot on the left side.

L

R

L

R

You should feel tall and proud as you follow the proper walking method. Begin to walk everywhere this way and you will perfect the way you walk. Just keep in mind that the way you walk will also leave an impression and you want it to be the proper impact of who and what you are.

It might be helpful if you can see some of the common errors in walking. Maybe this will encourage you to work hard at correcting the way you walk. Just like the way you speak, the way you walk will either attract or detract. You can't make it happen overnight, but with practice and concentration your walk will improve.

Take the time now to review the diagrams that follow and read the explanations of improper walking methods carefully. This is the first step toward understanding why it is so important to walk properly.

CHEST WALK: The chest arrives first. You suspect her feet hurt because she comes down heavily on one side. As she moves forward she leans to the other side.

SWING WALK: Pelvic forward, arms swinging. Her gait appears as though her body can't keep up with her legs. Her torso and head are far behind her legs.

SLOUGH WALK: Head first, neck thrusting forward. She seems to be sniffing her way along. Her head thrusting forward has her off balance.

BOUNCE WALK: Rises on her toes, drops down on her heels. This has her bouncing instead of walking.

DUCK WALK: The tummy is thrust forward, the rearend is back. The resulting curve makes the walker appear back heavy. She waddles. This posture breaks the long line from heel to head. The walker looks shorter, stockier, more awkward.

If any of these areas describe how you feel when you "use" to walk, you can imagine why you did not feel good or look good as you moved along. Now that you know how you should walk, practice it repeatedly and record in your mind the feel of each part of your body as you walk properly. After you have done this, you now are ready to learn how to stand.

Good Posture Check

Head is erect, your chin parallel to the floor, feeling as if a string extends form the top of your head to the ceiling, pulling your head up.

Shoulders are back and dropped in a relaxed position as if the neck is extending its full length.

Chest is held high as though your chest is lifting up and out.

Waist is stretched long as though you are standing taller.

Stomach is held in as if a wide metal ring is around squeezing it.

Buttocks are tucked under by tipping the pelvic bone forward and up as if a weight is settling down on your hips and you are not tipping the pelvic bone.

Joints are relaxed, elbows are slightly bent, and your wrists held so that the palms turn in toward your body.

To begin learning the proper way to stand, try practicing following the instructions below.

Left Stance Position:

- Place your feet about two inches apart.
- Place the toe of the right foot even with the left arch.
- Rest most of the body weight on the front (left) foot.
- Raise the heel of the right foot so that only the ball of the foot is on the floor.

- Relax and bend the right knee slightly.

- Rotate right heel in toward left foot till it is at a 45-degree angle (half a right angle). The heel of your left foot is now almost touching your right instep.

- Place your weight evenly between both feet

L

R

LEFT
BASIC STANCE

Look in the mirror and see how graceful and gently curved your legs appear in this proper standing position. Look at the diagram. As you look in a mirror, does your stance match that shown?

Right Stance Position

- Place your feet two inches apart.

- Place the toe of the left foot even with the right arch.

- Rest most of the body weight on the front (right) foot.

- Raise the heel of the left foot so that only the ball of the foot is on the floor.

- Relax and bend the left knee slightly.

- Rotate the left heel in toward the right foot till it is at a 45-degree angle (half a right angle or if your legs are heavy, adjust them more like the diagram). The heel of your right foot is now almost touching your left instep.

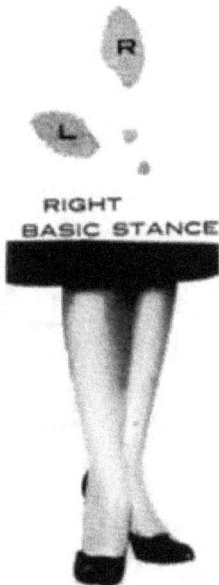

RIGHT
BASIC STANCE

In practicing the basic stance your weight should be evenly distributed on both hips and your hips turned slightly in the direction that your back foot is pointing. Keep your shoulders and head facing forward.

Practice shifting from right to left stances in front of a mirror. Be sure to keep knees close together and relaxed. The placement of your feet must always be coordinated with the good posture position of the upper body.

To walk into your basic stance, you would step back several feet from the mirror. Start walking forward on left foot, then right foot, then left. Place the right foot at an angle and bring the left foot in front of it, toe pointing straight ahead, in the left basic stance position.

To walk into the right basic stance, take a few steps and put your left foot at an angle and bring your right foot in front of it into the right basic stance position. Toe pointing forward. If you need to, review the walking diagrams as you combine them with the left and right stance. Now practice walking into the right and left positions until both are completely natural.

What To Do With Your Hands While Standing

If you are holding something you don't have to worry about those dangling hands, but if not, what can you do with your hands? Look over the following so that you won't appear like someone who is disconnected at the wrist.

METHOD ONE: Always put those elbows in close to your sides. This gives you a slimmer, trimmer silhouette. Press the forearm of one arm lightly against your waist with palm up, wrist and fingers relaxed. Allow the other arm to hang freely at your side or clasp the wrist of one hand lightly with the fingers of the other with palms up. Keep your elbows in at your side.

METHOD TWO: For a more poised hands at sides stance, let your arms hang easily, brush inside of wrists along body. This will help you avoid the awkward out-turned knobby wrist. But if you step out of the motionless basic stance position, do be sure that your arms swing (slightly) free, or you will look like a mummy with strapped arms.

METHOD THREE: With arms close at sides, forearms extended across in front of waist. Thumb of one hand rests lightly on tip of palm of other hand. Palms drop out openly, easily relaxed and down.

Don't be a finger, ring, knuckle, or wrist twister. If you can't control nervous finger fidgeting, put your hands behind your back and fidget where no one can see you. When you get nervous, hold onto yourself firmly with one hand circling the other wrists.

Practice these arm positions along with your basic stances. At first, they may feel unnatural and uncomfortable, but with practice will seem very natural to you.

Turning

Yes, there's more! You may want to walk forward or turn around when leaving your basic standing position. To do either you need to shift your weight to the back foot and always start with your forward foot.   If you are simply walking forward, there is no problem.   If you are turning around, you execute a graceful maneuver known as the Half Pivot.   Here's how to make that turn:

1)   Take the basic left standing position.
2)   Step forward onto your left foot, pointing your toe slightly to the left and shifting your body weight to this foot.
3)   Now place right foot in front of your left so the heel just barely grazes the toe of the left.   Your right foot points straight ahead.
4)   Rise imperceptibly on the toes of both feet and turn left until facing in the other direction.   You must

turn the upper half of the body ever so slightly in the direction you wish to move.

Properly performed, you will find yourself standing in the left basic stance again, only facing the other way. Eyes and head should always be kept raised while executing this motion and the turn should be done with the least lift and force to do it smoothly.

The right turn would be done opposite of the left. Practice left and right turns until you can do them naturally and with ease.

To have good posture you must have a strong back. If your back is weak or you feel any pain when getting into your perfect posture stance, you need to work on this. Practice the following exercise until you strengthen your back so that when you stand up straight you feel as good as you look.

- First you need to stand with your back against a wall with shoulders and hips touching it.

- Lift your rib cage up and out by pulling up through your waist.

- Tuck your buttocks under and bend your knees slightly.

- Come out of the stance and go through the steps again until your body is in the perfect posture position.

Practice this repeatedly. Keep practicing each day and your body will feel comfortable in this position. This exercise will give you the feel of perfect posture while standing while it continues to strengthen your back muscles.

Along with standing, you need to learn how to sit gracefully. To sit gracefully your body should be erect, but not stiff. It is important that you master the technique of properly sitting. You should practice this until you do it with ease. Remember that chair styles will vary, needing you to adjust the routine to compensate for the different chair styles.

Sitting Properly

Now that you know how to walk, you're going to learn how to sit properly. Look at the two diagrams for sitting that appear at the end of this lesson and do the following:

- Walk up to any chair, holding your best posture. Pivot into a basic stance position so that your back leg brushes against the chair seat. You can feel where the seat is, and you won't need to look for it.

- Now slide your back foot under the chair two or three inches. Then lower yourself into the seat. Keep your head erect and your back straight. Almost all your weight is carried by the thigh of your back leg.

Maintain your balance and don't flop into the chair with a bang. The reason for sliding one foot under the chair is to help you maintain a center of balance.

Practice gauging the chair height with your calf. You must slip your foot back under the chair to rise or sit down while holding an erect posture. Practice sitting down with all your weight on the back leg. Raise the other leg off the floor an inch or so as you practice. You will of course have to modify this sitting with various chairs and sofas. The deeper the seat, the further forward you will have to sit when you first lower yourself into place. Or, if the chair is built solid to the floor, you will be unable to place your back foot under the chair but move it as close to the front of the chair as you can and sit down further forward. Once you have managed to perch on the edge of the chair, simply lift your weight slightly and slide back.

Try not to use your hands when you lift your weight. If, however, the chair surface is too rough to allow gently sliding back, lift yourself slightly by placing your hands, flat on the seat of the chair, close to your sides, then slide back.

To rise from a chair, simply reverse the sitting procedure.

- Unnoticeably slide one foot back under the chair

before rising.

- Keep torso and head erect and poised. Do not shove up with derriere, do not push up with chair arms.

- Lift yourself gracefully and in one easy motion, with your back leg muscles doing the work.

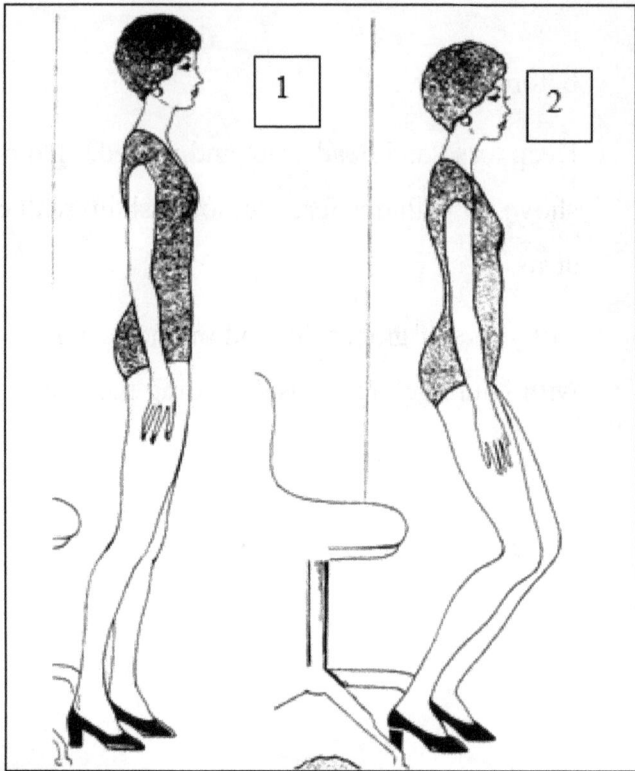

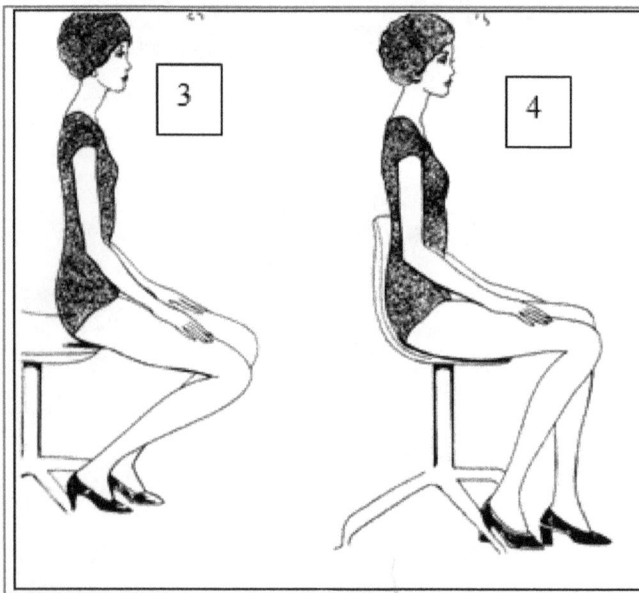

Legs And Feet While Sitting.

While sitting you arrange your legs at a slight angle to the chair. This will give a more fluid line to the body. You don't want to look like a frightened little girl on her first day at school with your hands folded primly and your feet set straight in front of you. There's a little "curve" strategy here. When you move your legs a little to right or left your legs appear shapely.

You may cross your ankles or knees. If you decide to cross your legs at the knee, cross them only above the knees not directly on the knees. And be sure your skirts are long enough to cover your knees. If your legs are heavy, cross just the ankles.

- Never sit with your legs stretched out in front of you like an old man. Sitting on the ground or on the beach at picnics, you will look composed if you fold your legs to one side.

  Your good posture habits should be so much a part of you that you can just relax and let your subconscious mind police your standing, sitting, and walking.

  Hands While Sitting.

The more relaxed and quiet your hands look, the
better. Let one hand rest easily in the other on your lap,
palms up. Put your hands into any position that is
comfortable and relaxed looking.

Proper Placement Of Your Hands

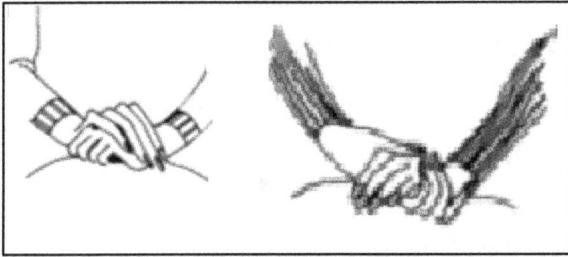

Skirt When Sitting

The less fuss you make over your skirt the better.
Never clutch your skirt, or tug at it. Look over the
following for suggestions:

Slim Skirt: You may have to sit a little more
forward in the chair to keep your knees discreetly covered.

Full Skirt: Place your hand behind you and
grasping the center back of the skirt, bring it out to one side
before you sit down.

- When sitting you need to avoid the square line of knees together, hands in lap, feet together at center.
- If you have heavy legs never cross them above knees. If your legs are thin and shapeless, avoid the greater leg show of legs crossed at knee.
- Avoid slouching on a bench or stool. The back should remain erect no matter what you sit on.
- Do not smooth skirts, tug at clothing, fidget with hands, pluck at jewelry, pat hair, or clench hands into fists.

Modeling Techniques

Do not forget that your state of mind controls your body. Your body is what your clothes hang on and if your posture is elegant then the dress you are wearing will reflect the same image.

You must have inner assurance before you can move elegantly. Once you have mastered perfect posture and feel elegant within yourself, you need to next work on the basics of modeling routines. You are about to learn there is one more factor you need to consider. It's the "art" of pivoting!

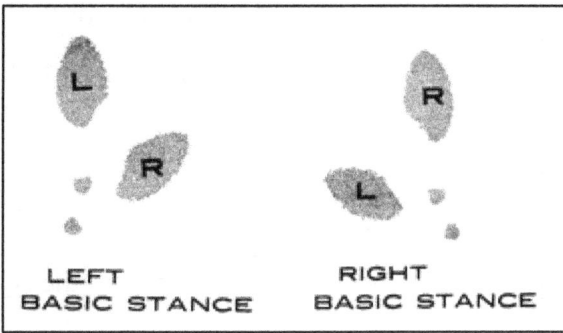

LEFT
BASIC STANCE

RIGHT
BASIC STANCE

Pivoting

Along with getting into your basic stance positions, as a model you will need to learn how to perform pivots. Outlined below are the pivots you will need in doing your modeling routines. The instructions and diagrams will help you master pivoting if you practice them faithfully.

Positioning From Left Basic Stance:

- Place your feet two inches apart.

- Place the toe of the right foot even with the left arch.

- Rest most of the body weight on the front (left) foot.

- Raise the heel of the right foot so that only the ball of the foot is on the floor.

- Relax and bend the right knee slightly.

- Rotate right heel in toward left foot till it is at a 45-

degree angle (half a right angle). The heel of your left foot is now almost touching your right instep.

Positioning from Right Basic Stance

- Place your feet two inches apart.

- Place the toe of the left foot even with the right arch.

- Rest most of the body weight on the front (right) foot.

- Raise the heel of the left foot so that only the ball of the foot is on the floor.

- Relax and bend the left knee slightly.

- Rotate the left heel in toward the right foot till it is at a 45-degree angle (half a right angle). The heel of your right foot is now almost touching your left instep.

TIPS

- Place your weight evenly on both hips and your hips turned slightly in the direction that your back foot is pointing. Keep your shoulders and head facing forward. Remember the good posture position of the upper body and check each area. See how graceful and gently curved your legs look. Place your right foot diagonally at the toe of the left foot. If you are in the correct position you will see that your right knee is actually hiding your left knee. This is your starting pose.

- If you were to increase the degree of the right heel to 90 degrees, you will notice that this movement shifts your back leg directly behind the front leg-- giving an almost bird-like appearance. This will hide any excess weight on your legs. Bringing your back foot to more of an angle will also automatically turn your hips more to the side, giving a slimmer, trimmer front view.

Half Pivot

The first pivot you will learn is what is known as the half pivot. You should practice the following instructions until you can do it in your sleep.

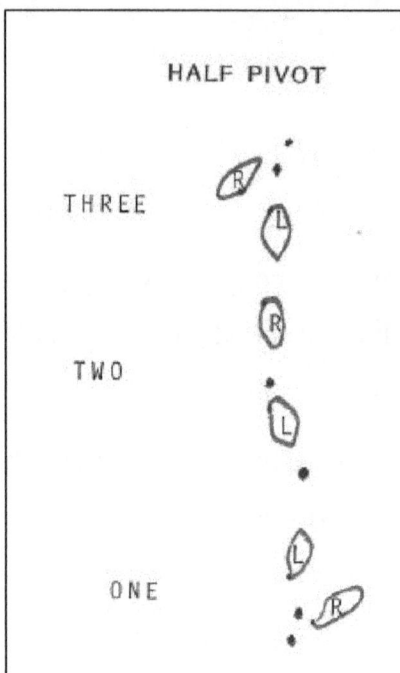

HALF PIVOT

THREE

TWO

ONE

- Take the basic left standing position. Step forward onto the left foot, pointing the toe slightly to the left.

- Keep eyes and head raised during the execution of this motion and use minimum lift and force.

- Shift body weight to left foot.

- Now place right foot in front of the left foot so the heel just barely grazes the toe of the left foot.

- Right foot should be pointing straight ahead.

- Rise imperceptibly on the toes of both feet and turn left until facing in the other direction.

- Turn the upper half of the body ever so slightly in the direction you wish to move.

- You should be standing in the left basic stance position once again but facing the other way.

- Now your half pivot is complete.

To do the **RIGHT HALF PIVOT**, follow the procedure, beginning in the left basic stance and leading with the left foot.

Quarter Pivot

If you want to turn facing either to the left or the right from a basic standing position and not completely around, you do a quarter pivot in the direction you wish to face.

QUARTER PIVOT

THREE

TWO

ONE

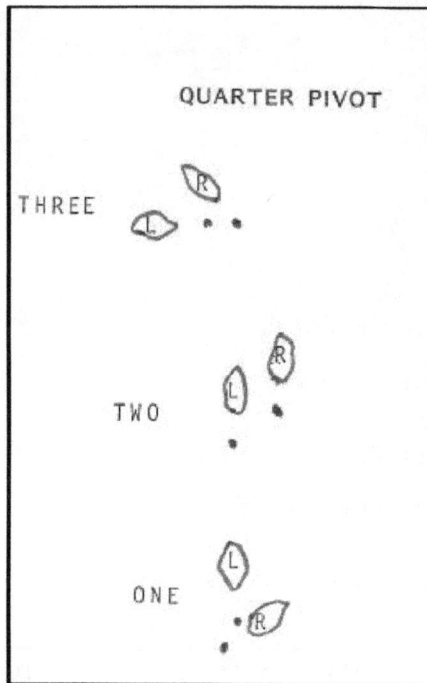

Left Quarter Pivot

- From a left basic stance take a short step forward with your left foot, keeping the toe pointing straight ahead.

- Step forward with the right foot, placing the heel of the right foot even with the instep of the left foot. Feet should be two inches apart.

- Shift your weight to the balls of your feet, lifting your heels slightly off the floor

- Turn to the left

- Your feet will again be in a left basic stance

position.

To do the **RIGHT QUARTER PIVOT**, follow the same procedure, beginning in the right basic stance, and leading with the right foot.

Full Pivot

You will be doing two half-pivots in the same direction to execute a full pivot or complete turn. You will also be coordinating your hand and arm movements with your feet placements.

- Stand in a basic stance, with your arms hanging loosely at your sides, elbows relaxed and close to your waist, writs lightly pressing against your body.

- Step forward, pointing your toe in the direction you are going to turn, and slowly bring your hands in

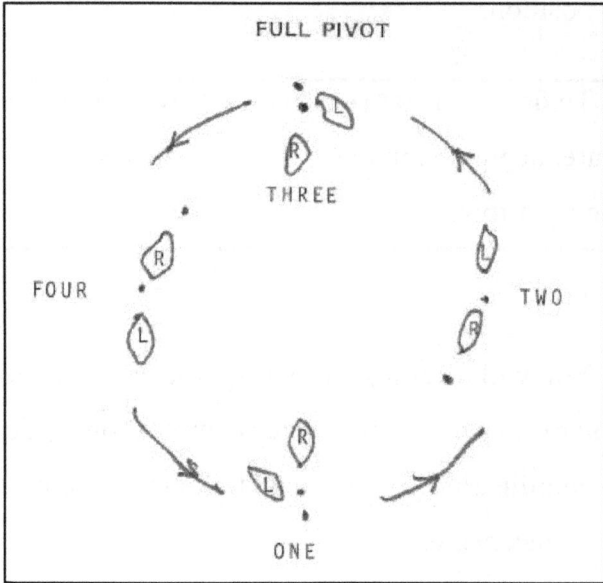

FULL PIVOT

THREE

FOUR

TWO

ONE

front of you, palms facing, but not touching, fingers in a gracefully curved position.

- Take the second step in the pivot routine and while you shift your weight to the balls of the feet, begin raising your hands to chest level.

- Turn on the balls of your feet and bring your elbows up and out at chest level, fingertips of your hands

barely touching.

- When your feet are in a basic standing position in the opposite direction, your forearms and hands are a graceful line across your chest.

- This completes half the routine.

- Now step out from this basic stance in the first step of the second half pivot, pointing your toe in the direction you are going to turn, and drop your elbows to your sides.

- Take the second step, and as you begin shifting your weight to the balls of the feet, bring your arms down loosely to your sides, palms turned toward your body, and lightly brushing against your thighs.

Stage Performances

There are usually four types of raise stage performances used in the fashion industry. It is important that you learn how to perform each to be a good fashion model. Along with the for types of performances, there are usually three types of stage surfaces. The stage types are as follows:

<u>Straight:</u>

The stage is usually a big square. The entrance is at the center back, with the audience seated at the right. You exit on the opposite end at the left. In using the full surface, you can perform the Inverted "V" or the "V" routine. The "Y" routine will also suffice.

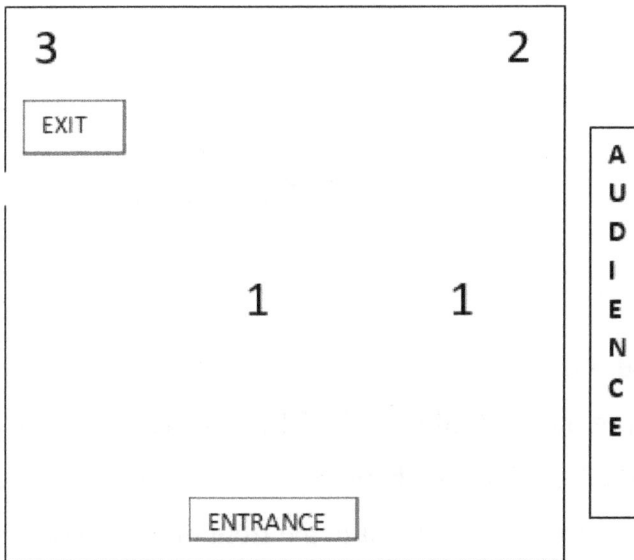

Inverted "L"

The stage is laid out like an upside down "L" and would appear reversed. You enter on the front of the tail of the "L". The audience would be on your right and at the top of the "L". You would exit at the same point you entered but using the back of the tail of the "L".   The "Y" the "T" or Inverted "V" routine works best on this stage.

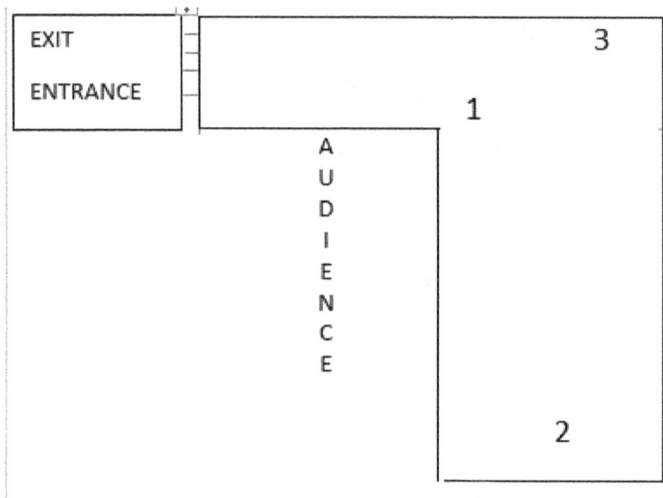

```
┌──────────────┬─┬──────────────────────────────┐
│  EXIT        │ │                          3   │
│              │ │                              │
│  ENTRANCE    │ │              1               │
├──────────────┴─┴──────────────┐              │
│                         A      │              │
│                         U      │              │
│                         D      │              │
│                         I      │              │
│                         E      │              │
│                         N      │              │
│                         C      │              │
│                         E      │              │
│                                │              │
│                                │         2    │
│                                └──────────────┘
```

The "T":

The stage is laid out like a fat "T". You would enter at the back of the cross of the "T". The audience would be seated on the left, right and bottom of the "T". You exit at the same point you entered, but in the front of the cross of the "T". The "T", "V" and Inverted "V" routines work best on this stage.

```
┌──────────┐─────────────────────────────────────┐
│ ENTRANCE │                                      │
│          │       1                 2            │
│ EXIT     │                                      │
└──────────┘──────┐                 ┌─────────────┘
           A      │        3        │ A
           U      │                 │ U
           D      │                 │ D
           I      │                 │ I
           E      │                 │ E
           N      │                 │ N
           C      │                 │ C
           E      │        4        │ E
                  └─────────────────┘
                      AUDIENCE
```

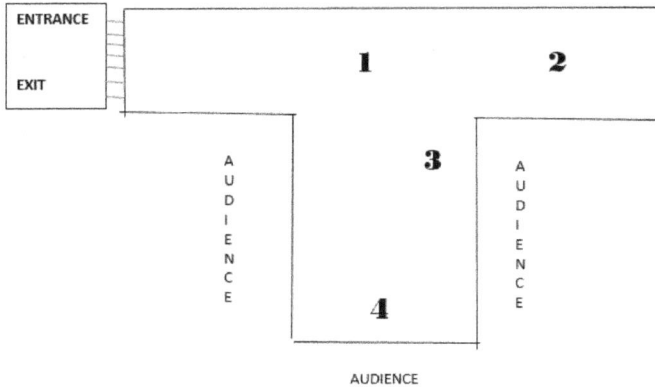

The above are the basic stage layouts. Now, by referring back to the layouts, you can match the following routines to the different stage types. It is important to not only know the various stage types, but the proper routines to start.   The three types of stages are diagrammed below showing the position you should be at to perform each part of the routines.

The "T"

- Begin the "T" routine by standing in a basic stance at the bottom of the stage steps.

- Walk up the steps and execute a full pivot as you step onto the stage.

THE "T"

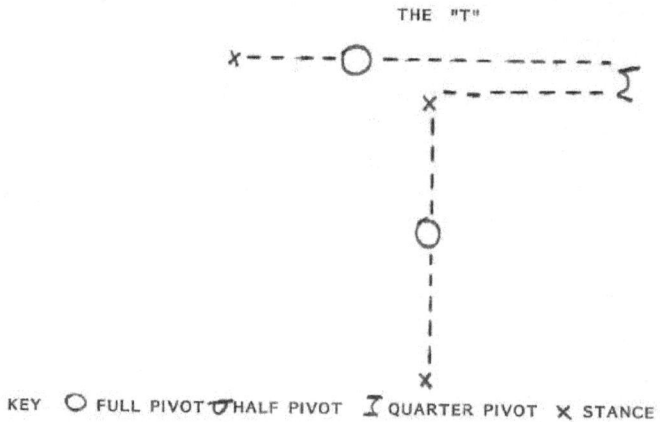

KEY ◯ FULL PIVOT ʊ HALF PIVOT ⫯ QUARTER PIVOT ✗ STANCE

- Walk across the back of the stage to the opposite side and execute a half pivot. You are now facing back the way you came.

- Walk back half way to center stage and take a basic stance, facing front. You have drawn the horizontal line of the capital "T".

- From your basic stance position, wall to the center stage front and execute a full pivot.

- Descend the steps and walk into a basic stance.

The "V"

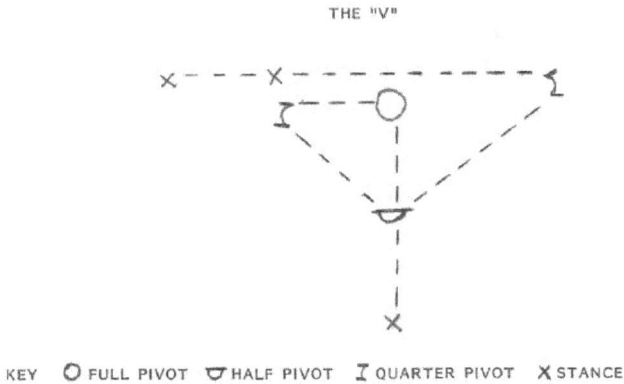

KEY   O FULL PIVOT   ▽ HALF PIVOT   Ɪ QUARTER PIVOT   X STANCE

-

- Stand in a basic stance at foot of steps. Ascend steps and walk into a basic stance at top of steps, side back of stage.

- Walk across to the opposite side of stage and execute a quarter pivot. You are facing the center of the stage.

- Walk to center front and execute a quarter pivot.

- Walk to side back of stage and execute a quarter pivot. You are now in the same spot on stage as when you began your routine and you have drawn the "V". You are facing the center back of the stage.

- To complete the routine, walk to center back of stage, and execute a full pivot.

Page 51 of 178

- Walk down center to front of stage, descend steps and walk into a basic stance at foot of steps.

The Inverted "V"

- Stand in a basic stance at bottom of stage steps.

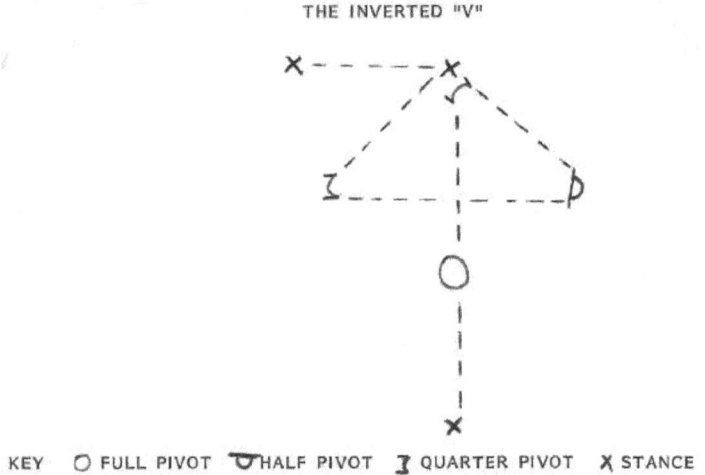

THE INVERTED "V"

KEY   ○ FULL PIVOT   ↻ HALF PIVOT   Ɫ QUARTER PIVOT   X STANCE

-

- Walk up steps and into a basic stance in the center back of stage facing front.

- Walk to side of middle stage and execute a quarter pivot. You are now facing the opposite side of stage.

- Walk across stage to opposite side and execute a quarter pivot.

- Walk to center back of stage and execute a quarter pivot. You are now facing front and have completed the inverted "V"

- To complete the routine and walk off stage, wall to center front of stage and execute a full pivot.

- Descend steps and walk into a basic stance.

The "Y"

- Begin in a basic stance position at the foot of the steps.

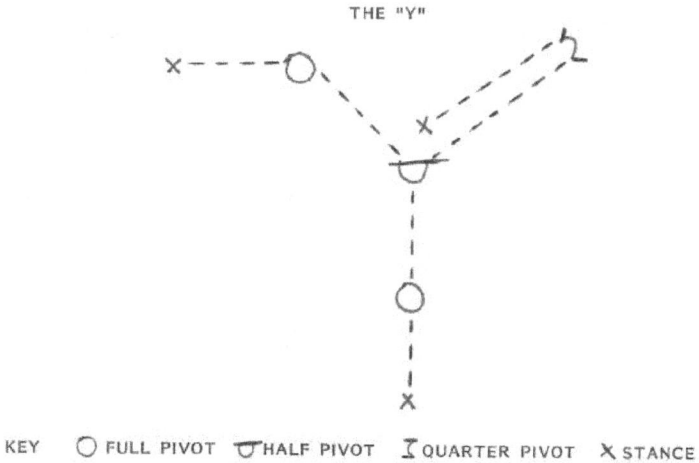

THE "Y"

x - - - -O

X

O

X

KEY   ◯ FULL PIVOT   ⊍ HALF PIVOT   ꟾ QUARTER PIVOT   ✗ STANCE

-

- Ascend the steps and execute a full pivot as you step onto the stage.

- Walk forward to the center middle of the stage and execute a half pivot.

- Walk to the opposite side of the stage back and execute a half pivot. You are now facing the center middle of the stage.

- Walk back to center middle stage and walk into a

basic stance, facing forward.

- Walk to center front and execute a full pivot.

- Descend steps and walk into a basic stance at the foot of the steps.

To start a successful performance on stage you need to remember that a beautiful walk is achieved through posture and balance. Posture and balance do not happen by accident, they are acquired through training and regular exercise. No matter what shape you are in, you will need to stick to a regular exercising program to keep your body flexible and healthy.

The Tools Of The Trade

Models who are poised and confident will often give the impression that their great look is something so real, so natural they must have been born with it. This is generally not true. Poise, confidence, and style are acquired skills and I can't say this enough. Any famous model has a lot in common with a dancer or an athlete--the better trained the person is, the easier the performance seems to be. So, to help you in reaching your modeling goal, you need to learn the basics and understand the language.

Attitude

Attitude is the winning quality toward success. When you wake up in the morning and feel absolutely terrible, your entire day becomes negative. On the other hand, when you wake up with a cheerful disposition and energetic movements, observe how the people around you are affected. A great attitude seems to rub off on all who come in contact with you.

The person who excels on a shoot or set, is the person who realizes she belongs there. When the call comes, it means you have been selected to do the photo session or commercial. It is your show and you should feel it, act it and do it. Remember that you have helped to create the excitement being generated.

Attitude is the one area of your life of which you have complete control. You should control your mood and never allow a bad attitude into your career.

The Approach

To enter the field of print, television, and runway, you will need to contact your local advertising agencies. Call and ask to speak with the art director of the agency. Introduce yourself and tell them you would like to send a resume and a headshot for local work. Never go into detail about your-self over the phone; you will be taking too much of their time.

If you are unable to speak to the art director, take their name and address and mail them your headshot and resume package. Contact your local department stores and again ask for either the advertising manager or the fashion coordinator. Tell them you would like to send a headshot and resume for local work. Local photographers also use models. Contact them and send a resume and headshot package.

Preparation

Organization is the key to success. The day before your modeling assignment, get detailed directions and even consider taking a trial run if necessary. Of utmost importance, never arrive late to your modeling assignment.

A good rule to live by is to try to arrive at least 15 minutes prior to the assigned time. Information on directions can be obtained by calling the local Chamber of Commerce or even the Police Department.

Concerning the assignment, be prepared by always having two of everything--two pairs of tights, stockings, pantyhose. Also take along cosmetics, toothpaste, brush and comb, hairspray, hairpins, barrettes, ribbons, shoes, and a change of clothes. For energy, take a Bee Pollen tablet before going and extra for later, or keep a granola bar or candy bar and something to drink between shoots.

Have everything packed the day before. Look each item over to be sure they do not require any repairs. Everything should be neatly pressed and clean.

The Call

You have made contacts with various agencies, department stores, manufacturers, and photographers. Now comes the waiting game and the follow up calls. When you get that first call you are going to be excited so plan now to be sure that you don't overlook getting the important information. Keep a pad by the phone and the following list near the pad.

You should know the answers to the following questions:

1.   Time.
2.   Place.
3.   Mood or clothes.
4.   Brief on location--get directions if needed.
5.   Brief on set.
6.   Confirmation of appointment by yourself.

The call can be informative and an asset to your success, or if you are over excited and not prepared, you could come away from the call unhappy, confused or discouraged.

Remember, treat all calls as if it were the big one. It could very well be. The call is the reward for the professional way you have sent out resumes and headshots to the right places and to the right people. Success is not an accident, success is planning and working on your plan.

Dress And Appearance

To start any photo session, you must be extremely well groomed. To help you achieve your goal, use the following as your check list before going out the door.

- Wash, condition, set and style your hair.

- Make sure you get enough rest so that you arrive with eyes clear and sparkling.

- Make sure that all your personal hygiene routines are handled properly.

- Give yourself enough time to apply your make up perfectly.

- Try to save time to exercise so that you will be alert and ready for the interview.

- Gather all your modeling tools the day before.

- Take a trial run to the location and leave in plenty of time so you don't arrive flustered.

- Be calm, cool, and collected so that you don't end up perspiring.

Additionally, pay particular attention to hair sprays that do not flake or build up. Should you have these problems, you may want to select a men's hair spray for finer hair, thus allowing you the security of knowing you will not have build up. Since your cosmetics will play a very important part of your photo session and what cosmetics you use will depend upon what the shot calls for, you should always be prepared. It is gratifying to look as close to natural as possible. To help mother nature, you must stay in the confines of earth tones (browns), soft blushes, and glosses for lips.

Remember, always be prepared for anything. But above all, start out clean, fresh, and natural. Let the photographer tell you what he needs changed after you arrive.

It's easier to add to, than to remove too much of anything.

The Tools

The following items are a must for models to have prepared well in advance of making that first call.

Resume or Biography

Your resume or biography should consist of 100 to 300 words that best describe your activities, credits (when and for whom you have modeled) any plays performed, talent, awards and past titles, if any. Also include future desires and goals. This should be laid out following the same format as the resume instructions given in the preceding chapter. If possible, you should include two phone numbers where you can be reached and a fax number, if you have one.

If you must go beyond the word length, make sure that you are not over emphasizing points, but need more words to paint a total picture of your accomplishments.

Vital Statistics

Along with your resume you should have a sheet that covers your statistics. Statistics in the modeling world deals with your physical make up. You can provide this in a format similar to the one below.

The statistics as well as the resume represents the first introduction of you. Therefore, it should be neatly typed with no spelling errors. Don't rush through the preparation or you will be sorry later if you left out any pertinent information that might have gotten you the job. So knowing this take the time now to plan it out and present yourself as professionally as possible.

VITAL STATISTICS

SKYE CHAMBERS

225 Nice Street

Pleasanton, CA 94002

918-555-5151

918-555-6275

918-555-9171 (fax machine)

AGE: 24

HEIGHT: ....5' 10"

WEIGHT: ....125 lbs.

BUST: ....34"

WAIST: ....24"

HIPS: ....34"

HAIR COLOR: Auburn

EYE COLOR: Green

SKIN TONE: Tan

SIZES

DRESS: ....7 Petite

SKIRT: ....7 Petite

SHIRT: 34

PANT: 8

JACKET: 34

SHOE: 7 1/2

Headshot

An 8 x 10 headshot of you looking directly into the camera should be part of your package. This shot is always asked for by photographs and they usually want it in black and white. You can also have a color headshot, but usually if a major studio, television network or whoever, wants to see you in living color, they will ask for you in person or state they prefer a color shot. This photo is the start of your portfolio.

Most modeling studios will want to sell you a composite. A composite is a group of pictures (usually a head-shot on the front and three poses on the back) with your modeling stats. They come in a size that is easy to mail out to prospective employers and can save you money in the long run since you will receive a bulk quantity to send out and have on hand for future mailings. Bear in mind thought that in the reproduction of an 8x10 photograph you may see distortions in the reprints.

Not so with a composite. For good quality reprints of a photograph, the cost can be steep, while composite reproductions are less expensive, but though you want to keep the price reasonable, you need to have good representation and that comes from your photographs.

The need for composites is always debatable in the industry. You will find that the jobs are just as readily obtained with the 8 x 10 headshot and the biography, as with the composite.

The Portfolio

The importance of a professional portfolio cannot be over-stated. It is the umbilical cord of the modeling world. Your material should be presented in a neat and organized way. If done properly, even a small beginning portfolio can be impressive if it has been carefully organized. There is only one type of portfolio. It is a flat case for carrying photographs, resumes, etc. It may be as large as 36 x 48 or as small as a photo album. Inside, plastic pages may be used to protect your photographs that should be 8 x 10 or larger. Don't put in contact sheets or anything to distract from the professional appearance of your portfolio.

If you have some excellent 5 x 7 shots, include them in a separate section in the back of the portfolio in an organized fashion. If the potential employer is interested he will go on to this section but should have captured your potential in the *first three pages*. Also, any clippings that you have of yourself in advertising advertisements or pageants can be included at the back of your composite in a neat and orderly fashion.

You should take care in arranging your pictures. The first three are the most important--the ones that show the most versatility and your abilities in different atmospheres should be considered for this position. The following photos should enhance the main three shots. As a rule of thumb, the first photo in your portfolio should be a black and white headshot, the following can be color or black and white.

Along with the quality of your portfolio, you need to present it to a prospective client in a professional manner. Presenting your portfolio to a potential employer is performed during the interview.

The Interview

An interview is a personality encounter. Enter in a confident manner and be positive about yourself and your work. You should walk in smiling. Once you have entered the room for the interview, you should extend your hand to introduce yourself. Grasp the interviewers hand in a firm handshake that transmits the message of your professionalism. While you shake the interviewer's, hand introduce yourself giving your first and last name. At this time, you should state if you represent yourself or are with an agency.

Allow the interviewer to show you to a chair or follow his directions to be seated. Once you are seated, gracefully open your portfolio and with a smile, walk over and hand it to the interviewer. You should then return to your seat and sit quietly, remaining calm while the interviewer looks over the contents of your portfolio.

If you are asked a question, be sure to talk with confidence and to the point. Don't rattle on as it will make the interviewer sense you are on edge. Do not talk about other agencies or answer any questions by responding with only a "yes" or "no". When you are signaled the interview is at an end, walk over to the interviewer and ask for your composite. You should allow the composite to rest on the desk while you remove a copy of your headshot, statistics sheet, and resume (or your composite). You should have two phone numbers on the resume for contact and if you have one, a fax number.

Once you have completed the interview process, the hard part comes. Never call the client to see if you got the job. They will call you if they are considering you for the assignment.

Types Of Modeling Jobs

There are basically three categories of modeling: *editorial, commercial, and runway*. Some models pursue modeling only in television commercials or magazine ads while others prefer the "steady job" atmosphere provided by retail or showroom modeling. Each specialized category of modeling demands special techniques and, therefore, special training.

There are certain basics which apply to all modeling. They must be learned first as in any other field. Once the basics are mastered, the aspiring model can be trained in one or more specialty areas. Very few models work in every specialized field. A model's ability to work in a certain field is dependent upon the model's type as well as age, height, weight, etc. But a model's natural talent and training can overcome not being the preferred type. This is particularly true if you are versatile enough to achieve the natural, real people look as well as the sophisticated people look. You have probably seen models who do both and not even been aware that you were seeing the same person in both advertisements. It's all a matter of knowing how to achieve different looks through hair styling and application of make-up. The same model who does the "real people" look cam restyle their hair, put on the high-fashion makeup and do catalog ads for Sears or Penny's. This comes with practice and using some of the techniques covered in the lessons.

So how do you decide what type of modeling is for you. Look at the following information which will help you make your decision.

Runway Modeling

Poise is your key quality.   Make sure your turns on the runway are extremely smooth and slow.   You must have what is called "TECHNIQUE"--the walks, turns and moves that show off the clothing.   Good eye contact with your audience is of the utmost importance and you must be in control of your runway.

Your hands and arms should be displayed well always.   The middle finger and ring finger should be close together with the hand slightly outward.   This will give you a polished look on the runway.   Models are like sales representatives; an amiable personality and an ability to work with others and take directions is essential.   If you are not professional, you will not be re-booked.

Showroom Modeling

Showroom modeling is runway modeling done by models employed directly by the apparel manufacturer.   It is their job to show the line to store buyers.   This is a steady type of modeling "9 TO 5".   The showroom model is paid every week, gets paid vacations, and other company benefits. To be a showroom model you need to be a true size. Extremely muscular or full-figures are not desirable for showroom modeling. This type model is usually the slim type. The main ingredient in this type of modeling is being able to "WORK WITH THE GARMENT" and show it off with the right mood and attitude to fit the clothing.

Retail Modeling

This is a form of runway modeling. The setting for the retail model is the large department store, the custom salon or the specialty store that carries name designer clothing. This is usually a "9 TO 5" job with all the benefits of full-time work. Some are hired on a part time basis, so they have free time to pursue other modeling specialties such as photographic or television modeling.

The runway modeling that we are most familiar with is fashion show modeling. This is a different style of modeling from either retail or showroom. They are more theatrical. They always feature theatrical lighting and exciting music. They are **A SHOW**.

Another area of retail modeling is the fragrance model. This type of modeling is the presentation of a fragrance to customers in a department store. The model is there representing the fragrance manufacturer. The job entails "live advertisement" of a product on a personal basis with each individual customer. Job assignments range around three to four-hour periods throughout the week. The individual is not an employee of the store but works on a "freelance" basis or through an agent.

Many are familiar with fashion shows put on by local department stores. There are many other fashion shows that the public has little knowledge of, those being trade shows and even restaurant showings.

Print Modeling

Print modeling involves having great eye contact and product appeal with the camera. Are you photogenic? On this type of work, photographers do not retouch photographs. They will not use a marginal model and take hundreds of pictures hoping to find the one good shot. They want models who look terrific every time.

You will need an outgoing personality. You will need to communicate special qualities of energy, enthusiasm, pleasure, enjoyment, sparkle, flare, and charisma. Whether you love the outfit or hate it, you must communicate total confidence.

Catalog and magazine layouts can be lengthy shots. You must take direction well. In the advertising profession, there is disagreement on whether to use illustration or photograph.   Some advertisers prefer photography because photographs give reality to the clothing.   Others prefer illustration because a drawing can add glamour to a garment.   Whether a photo or a drawing is used in the advertisement, a model often poses for it. The technique of the illustration model is quite different from that of the photographic model.   It is another specialty for which the serious model must become skilled through training.

The successful print model often works for only a small number of illustrators.   Once set up with a famous illustrator, the model can count on call backs.   With a small roster of steady clients, the model works in an easy and friendly atmosphere usually more relaxed than most photographic assignments.

Photographic modeling covers commercial print, editorial print, and catalog work. This is still photography. In still photography work, the ability to freeze without looking frozen is only one of the vital techniques that must be mastered.   Most catalog work is carefully posed, and the model must be able to hold a pose for minutes while the garment is adjusted, pinned, draped, and displayed exactly right for the camera.   While in editorial work the model must hit a variety of poses while the photographer pays less attention to the precise look of the garment than he would for catalog work. The key in still photography is to know your best look, be able to hold it, return to it if necessary, and look like you enjoy it. The best way to accomplish this is to feel the location of the hair, the jawbone, the eyes, the hand--everybody part individually and remember it.

Television Modeling

Depending on the type of involvement of the script, all the information in regard to print will apply to television. It is important to be able to take direction well. The areas of production time and budget money comes into play with television modeling. You will feel the pressures of trying to meet the requirements in a set amount of time--this is the separation point between a professional and an amateur model.

The most important fact about television modeling is that television needs the widest variety of *"Types"*. It is not limited to one certain look and there is a need for every height, weight, age, coloring, and style. The largest amount of money spent in television advertising is in the area of household products such as soap, deodorants, toothpaste, etc. You must look the part the instant you appear on the screen.

The need to know what type of modeling you will be doing is important. For instance, a product model who displays products of a quiz program is a fashion model. They are usually very pretty, young, and female. The height is unimportant, but grace and poise are a demand.

If you are to advertise a household product you may be typed as glamorous and even when doing the most unglamorous look. Age requirement may vary anywhere from infant to 80 years old. If you have a good voice quality and natural talent, then you may be able to do voice-over in announcements for radio or television commercials.

Television commercials you may find to be your best entree into features or television film or tape. The agencies often film or tape in Hollywood or New York, using top name production companies. Approximately 1,000 films are produced each year through nine major studios; however, only about 370 reach the commercial movie theater, or television stations.

Hand Modeling

Look at your hands. Outside of servicing you, hands can be beautiful and are often a part of modeling on their own. Thing of the hands you have seen in ads, flip through magazines and look at the hands as they hold a bottle of aspirin or lightly touch a brim of a hat. Notice how the camera focuses in on the object being held or touched. This is hand modeling.

There are no set rules in modeling your hands other than your fingers should appear relaxed and natural. Besides that, the hands need to appear graceful and well taken care of with no chip nail polish, skin soft and smooth, just like you learned in Chapter 9. If hand modeling is for you, make sure you take good care of your hands and wear gloves whenever you are immersing your hands in water or working in the garden. With proper care, there is no reason why you can't pursue a career in hand modeling. And extend that care to exercising your hands which will keep them looking graceful and relaxed. Once you have your hands in excellent shape, the following will help you in preparing for a career in hand modeling.

- Look through magazines, studying and practicing the placement of hands on the face, objects, hips, hat brims, etc. Cut out pictures of hand placements that you feel comfortable doing and keep them in a file.

- Remember when you go for the interview for the job you should have your hands and nails in perfect condition and be conscious of their movements and placement during the interview.

- It goes without saying that you should have photographs of your hands to show, and your composite should include a shot of your hands only. Use pastel nail polish on black and white shots, bold nail polishes for color shots.

There is a "lingo" to the business of hand modeling. In describing the main three fingers that you will use in holding objects for photographs it is important to learn the terms. Most photographers will instruct you using the following terms:

- The finger next to the thumb is referred to as the Index or Forefinger

- Your little finger is referred to as the Fifth or Pinkie finger

- The finger next to the little finger is referred to as the Ring finger

When it comes to the small items, placement of the fingers becomes all important. The reason for this is that the camera has too zoom in when you are holding a small object. So, to give you some pointers, along with looking at advertisements, remember the following:

- Place your thumb on the front of the object (toward

the camera), your index finger on the side of the object with a slight bend at the first knuckle (nearest the hand), and the balance of your fingers spread one inch apart, slightly bent (behind the object).

Another method of holding a small bottle would be to:

• Place the thumb on the left side of the bottle, the finger next to the "pinkie" on the other side of the bottle, and the remaining fingers close together in a straight and upward pose.

Fashion Show Routines

Fashion shows can be fun as well as demanding. When taking part in a fashion show for the first time you should do a basic routine of proceeding up the stairs with a straight back, thighs doing the work and feet straight ahead. Walk to the center of the stage always looking at the audience around you and keep your body relaxed. Acknowledge the presents of the audience on all sides of the runway as you proceed and never looking down at your feet. As you move around the stage, listen closely to the commentator who will help you focus on the details of the garment.

When you have completed your routine and the
commentator has concluded his description of the garment,
pivot to return to the entrance/exit area. Move gracefully
down the runway making eye contact with the audience and
again emphasize any parting garment details from the
commentator by looking or touching the garment. And
remember, to not exit until the commentator has completed
the description and keys you to leave the stage.

That's the basics, the point where you will start your
debut. Once you become familiar with the world of fashion
modeling you can work on enhancing your routine. That
usually starts once you know the standards of the stage
layouts. We will begin by describing the stages and the
modeling routines that work well on the stage type.
Following the stage descriptions you will find the details of
the routines.

Modelling Lingo

You can't make it if you don't understand the
language of the modeling world. The following are some
of the words you will need to be familiar with:

- CALL-BACK: Positive results on a casting
  call or a go-see

- CASTING CALL: A theatrical opportunity for a

possible acting job.

- COMMERCIAL MODEL: A model that is used for trade shows, demos, hosting, etc.

- COMPOSITE: A usually 8 1/2x5 1/2 heavy stock sheet to be forwarded to agencies interested in using models. A headshot is usually on the front with two to three shots on the reverse side along with model stats, address and phone number.

- CONTRACT: A legal and binding written agreement between any two parties.

- DUBBING: To add later to an already current commercial or to redo a present black and white video into color.

- DIRECTOR: An individual that is in total charge of a TV motion picture, commercial, special or major film and still photography.

- EDITORIAL MODEL: A high fashion model which appears primarily in up-scale newspapers and magazines.

- FREELANCE: An individual that works entirely on their own without the aid of a studio, agent or personal manager.

- GO-SEES: A modeling agency's directive for a

possible opportunity for a job.

- HEADSHOT: An 8 x 10 black and white photograph from the shoulders up preferably a direct look into the camera.

- INTERVIEW: The act of personally viewing close up of an individual that is applying for a particular position.

- NON-UNION:An organization for development of jobs which is totally directed without the aid of unions thus billing management.

- PRINT: Still modeling to be photographed, to be reprinted in a catalog, brochure, newspaper, magazines and point of purchase sales aides.

- PORTFOLIO: A collection of individual's professional photographs showing either past performances or a great variety of the individual.

- RESUME: Compiled information based on an individual's past performances and credits.

- RE-TAKE: The act of redoing a commercial or part until such part is deemed acceptable.

- RUNWAY: A raised, lighted stage with a maximum length of 25 feet by 8 feet wide. Or a high fashion clothing model who acts as a sales representative for the clothing manufacturer.

- SCRIPT: A presentation developed by writers to create an idea or story.

- SHOOT: A photo session.

- STATS: Statistics of an individual describing their height, weight, age, hair and eye color, etc.

- TV COMMERCIAL: A video taped model/actor promotion companies image and/or product.

- UNION: An organization of laymen developed to acquire rights and privileges of their individual industries.

- VIDEO: A taped filming of individuals or events which can be edited and utilized at a later date.

- VOICE ON CAMERA: A speaking part that is conducted by a live model and/or actor for commercial use.

Composites: Quality VS Quantity

Earlier I mentioned the composites and how this is sometimes used in place of a headshot, statistics sheet and resume. In presenting the composite I also mentioned that it was not as good as having the 8x10 photographs. But in some circles, the composite is looked at differently. To give you both sides of the coin, I share the following information with you.

Top modeling agencies stress the importance of putting together a composite/portfolio that includes one very important Ingredient--**Personality**! A composite should be produced to represent a *"visual statement"* that speaks for both the model and the photographer.   It is annoying when a modeling school works with a photographer to produce a boring, mass produced, look alike composite which lacks personality. Models need to gain experience. They cannot see what can be accomplished when they are not herded through a photo session. You should visit several reputable photograph studies to have your pictures taken and do this on an individual basis.

Beyond the importance of setting up a portfolio or composite, you have to get the photos out!   It's funny but there are models who purchase composites and then store them in their closet.   You won't hear of someone getting a modeling job who does this and it's hard to understand their reasons when there is a cost involved.   The fact is that if you pay money for something to help you do a job that you want to do, why not get the "tools" out and see if you can get some print work or television commercials.

A model who can distinguish between a composite with personality and one that was "mass produced" is one who will succeed. There are several ingredients necessary for a model to end up with a composite that speaks well of their modeling abilities and is representative of a good photographer.

The Model Must

- Know the photographer

- Communicate with the photographer

- Express details to the photographer that will uncover their personality

- Play an active role in planning the shoot.

A Good Photographer Must

- Know the model

- Communicate positively with the model

- Seek to produce a composite that shows a touch of class

- Plan before shooting

Agencies, Clients & Photographers

Now that you have gone to the expense of having pictures taken, having a composite printed, and a resume set up. What do you do next. First of all make sure you understand that you will need a black and white headshot, a resume, and a portfolio, or a composite and a portfolio. If you are sure you have all the tools of the trade it is time to take action. I could print a listing of who you should contact but that would limit you to very few areas, mainly local, as well as risk the chance that an agency had moved, or the contact person had changed. Therefore, I prefer to tell you how to go about getting your pictures out.

First, no matter where you live you should first go through the yellow pages of your telephone book and look under Advertisers, Photographers, Shopping Malls/Plazas. Then think of all the large department stores and local business that advertise. If you are interested in out-of-state or out of your city possibilities, go to the public library and look at the telephone books that they have there. Again go through the yellow pages and recall commercials you may have seen on television for other ideas for businesses that advertise.

Your next step will be to get recent issues of popular magazines (Redbook, Ladies Home Journal, Glamour, Ebony, etc.) and look at the credit pages for names of photographers, the department heads that may be interested in receiving your picture, etc.

In your search you will gather contact names, company names, addresses, and telephone numbers. After you have prepared the list you will begin contacting the agencies one at a time. In making the personal contact make sure you get all the pertinent information (what department you should send the information to, what will be required, the name of the contact person, double check the address and the spelling of words, names, etc.). Once this is done you will begin to send out your pictures. Try to determine who would be most interested, or the ones that you are most interested in working with and then mail these out first. Continue through your listing until you have sent each one the picture/composite/resume, etc. Then wait!

If you are really interested in getting your modeling career off the ground, this is the best way to go about it. It will take work and effort on your part, but the results are worth it.

LESSON 23:
THE WORLD OF PAGEANTS

Pageants are a way of expressing your true belief in you. A pageant can be any production on stage. Here we are mainly talking about a beauty pageant, but pageantry would also include musical presentations, theater performances, singing; to name a few. To participate in a pageant is a way of saying that you are confident and capable of portraying that confidence to everyone around you. But more so, it is a way of knowing if others really see you as having developed to your full potential. After all, when you enter a pageant you are going to be judged on your performance, intelligent responses to questions, and the overall way you look. That is not to say, as some may tend to disagree, that you must be beautiful. Instead, it is more of what and who you are and the image you portray. It is this image that is judged. If you are intelligent, know how to work with your personal attributes, and carry yourself proudly you can walk away as the winner. In other words, it will take more than beauty to win.

If pageants interest you it goes without saying that you need all the tools presented in the lessons. But additionally, you will need the tools that were presented in the chapter on modeling. So before you begin this chapter, make sure you have read the modeling chapter.

What Are Pageants

The original meaning of the word "pageant" has been extended over the years. Pageants began as entertainment, often in the open air, involving spectacles that were sometimes extravagantly devised and usually used as a means of expressing national, communal, or other kinds of group purpose or identify. Derived from the Latin word "pagina", "page", and essentially in its pre-modern manifestations considered to be a kind of illustration.

At one point in history parades and pageants became related phenomena, often one and the same thing, although a pageant might include events other than processions or omit them altogether. It was characteristic of pageantry, as it was of heraldry, to represent in symbolic form the various classes and castes of society. The common people would develop forms of pageantry that proclaimed their own interests, while the religious, merchants and ruling classes would produce other forms of pageantry, but of equally characteristic forms. Throughout the years thought, pageantry was thought of and used as a method of expressing national, communal, or other kinds of group purpose or identify.

To the original meaning of pageantry we add the ingredient of staging. Staging encompassed concrete shapes of a dramatic event. It embraced, the arrangement of words, performers, dance, music, setting, costume, makeup, lighting and other properties for maximum theatrical effectiveness. Throughout most of its history the theater has included all of the communal performing arts in a creative celebration of the richness of human activity as well as the aspirations of mankind. Costumes and makeup played a major role.

The original attire for stage was elaborate with the success of the production dependent in large measure on the designer's ability to understand and interpret the directors production concept, and also the symbolism of the performers presentation objectives. Theatrical makeup was initially considered to be the practice of painting, enhancing, or altering the face and body of the actor with cosmetics, plastic materials and hair. Later, theatrical makeup took on the additional meaning of not only makeup application but the collective term for the materials used in making up.

Actors have used makeup in the theater for a long period of time. Makeup was used to not only look their best and to help in transforming their appearance but also to ensure that they would be seen and recognized by the entire audience. How well an actor was seen depended upon the distance between them and the farthest spectator as well as the amount of available light. It was recognized that distances tended to blur the features, making recognition of the actors extremely difficult for the spectators.

Pageantry as we view it today takes its origin not only from pageants of old, but from staging techniques as well. As the actors had to learn their roles, the pageant contestant has to learn theirs. First of all they need to interpret the meaning of "beauty" as it relates to pageants. Beauty means not only outer, but inner beauty. In order to be a whole person you must have this special gift of inner beauty that was explained in the lesson on finishing touches. Inner beauty is being able to relate or conduct one's self in relationships with other people. In order to develop your inner beauty you must first learn to love yourself so that you become genuinely interested, caring, concerned and respectful of "You". Only through loving yourself can you learn how to love others.

Along with inner beauty you need to work on your poise, personality and charm.

<u>Poise</u>

Poise is an easy self possessed assurance of manner. It is graciousness and tact in coping and handling situations in a pleasant manner that allows you to interact well with other people. Not only is poise associated with manner, it is also part of the way you carry yourself. In this sense poise is the way you move and walk.

<u>Personality</u>

Personality is the quality or state of being a person. It is the ability to relate to other people with understanding and graciousness.

The development of your individual behavioral and emotional characteristics in a manner that reflects the best of you is the mark of a good personality. Personality then is summed up to reflect a distinction or excellence of personal and social traits.

<u>Charm</u>

Charm is a trait that allows an individual to fascinate, allure, or delight other individuals. It is a physical grace or attraction that provides the capability of pleasing, soothing, or delighting by having the ability to attract.

This is pageantry!

<u>Pageant Facts</u>

Pageants can be helpful in launching a modeling career. They can also be helpful in giving an individual confidence as it takes more than knowing how to model to be successful in the field of pageantry. It takes confidence! Confidence in knowing that you are the best you can be and really loving yourself in a way that shows in everything you do. People enter pageants for more reasons than just to win!

You may know about pageants or someone who has entered a pageant, but you may not be aware of what pageants are all about. In the pages that follow you will become familiar with the field of pageantry.

Pageants are fun as well as providing a worthwhile experience for the participant. There are pageants for every age group starting with birth and up to the age of senior citizens and beyond. Most are broken down into age categories of competition.

Why enter a pageant? If you want to increase your self confidence and encourage yourself to learn how to be the best you can be, then pageants can be beneficial to you. Here is an opportunity to present yourself at your very best from head to toe. From input obtained from peers, judges and pageant directors, you will receive helpful hints on hair style, makeup, modeling, clothes, etc. All of this information can help you not only when you are competing in pageants, but in your everyday life as well.

Pageants usually judge an individual on their beauty, poise, personality and charm. Within these categories you are being judged on:

1) The suitability of your hairstyle to the clothes you wear.

2) How well you have applied your makeup (if required)

3) The suitability of the clothing you have chosen.

4) The care you have taken with keeping your body in top physical condition.

Usually there will be other areas of competition that goes beyond the standard judging of beauty, poise and personality. You may find that a pageant also offers competition in the following areas:

1) Talent (a timed presentation of a routine in dance, singing, playing of musical instruments, etc.)

2) Photogenic (the judging of how well you photograph in a picture)

3) Speech (presentation of a timed speech presentation whose topic is general), etc.

4) Grade point averages (the judging of your grade average you have attained in your schooling.

5) Community involvement (judging on how active you are in your community in the area of volunteer work)

6) Personal Interview (judging done on information supplied on the application and responses to questions.)

Prizes for pageants range from the traditional pageant banner, crown, and flowers, to scholarships, money, tv's, fur coats, etc.

Once you have made the decision to enter a pageant it is recommended that you first try and take the opportunity to sit in the audience and find out the pertinent facts.

1)   The credentials of the judges

2)   Clothing attire required

3)   Length of time required for the pageant

4)   The age group you will compete in (ranges in ages of contestants

5)   The general size (as to contestants participating)

6)   The type of prizes being awarded, as well as the cost to enter.

For a starting point, the following information on various pageants has been accumulated. There is a sample listing of pageant groups that I am familiar with supplied later in this section. Since pageants, like anything else may change from year to year, this is just a reference area that you can build upon a starting point to give you some ideas as to how to begin and follow through on you idea to enter a pageant.

Preparation For Pageants

Before you make a decision to enter a pageant, it is best to attend as a member of the audience so that you are aware fully prepared for the competition. Once you have all the information that was outlined above, you are ready to make the decision to enter.

It may be beneficial to make a list of items that you or friends have asked about a certain pageant and take it with you. Once the pageant is over, try and see if you can get the answers to your questions. When you are satisfied, you can enter knowing exactly all that is expected of you and what you can expect from the pageant.

How many times have you heard parents and friends say that they cannot understand why a particular contestant was selected over the others. No one but the judges can say for sure, but at the base of the contestant winning is her ability to demonstrate her self-confidence while on-stage. She moves with an ease that shows her respect for herself and all that she has mastered in her self-development. That makes a winner, not outer, but inner beauty.

Many months and often years of preparation is at the base of an excellent on-stage performance. And just as many months goes into the preparation for the personal interview segment of a pageant. No one wins without confidence or preparation. Remember that!

It is the minority of contestants who win with just basic modeling training. And even less who win through family and friendly advice. It is important that it first be understood that the pageant contestant is a trained professional who knows exactly what works and what does not. A contestant who is serious about winning will hire a coach or attend pageant training sessions. Private training will cover all aspects of this book because it takes total self-development for an individual to meet the criteria of pageantry.

The training needs to cover a full analysis of the individual to focus on strong points and weak points. The trainer and contestant become intimately involved through the sessions that delve into stress, overcoming energy drainage either during the training or in pageants, the art of projecting vitality, the value of leaving a good lasting impression, the art of body language, shaking hands, answering questions during interviews, and most importantly the art of total acceptance of a peer's winning.

Is It Exploitation

But there is something more that the contestant in a beauty pageant has to accept and overcome; the adverse publicity given on beauty pageants.

Everyone who is involved in pageants has been confronted at one time or another with the question, "Why do you enter beauty pageants"? or "Don't you feel exploited by being a part of a beauty pageant"?

Let me just share the following with you that may help you understand. When the pageant is over and the winner is on stage having her picture taken, most of the other contestants have congratulated her and are on their way home to share with their families and friends what they have learned and how much fun the pageant was to them. At the same time these same contestants begin plans to enter their next pageant and often encourage their friends to also enter. Why, because there is more to gain from a pageant than being chosen the queen.

These contestants learn how to set a goal and how to achieve a goal. They also learn how to develop to their full potential through self examination. Then there are the benefits of learning to keep their poise during stressful situations, how to take constructive criticism, how to positively relate to people of different backgrounds, how to discipline themselves, how to prepare and carry through on an interview, how to prepare and present a talk before the public, and how to develop a healthy sense of competition.

I could go on and on, but I think you can see that pageantry not only develops an individual to succeed in a beauty pageant, but also helps them to succeed in "life" the right way.

Determining The Legitimacy Of A Pageant

Once you have decided to explore the exciting world of pageantry, you must not walk into the arena blind. You need to understand what is expected of you as a contestant, and what you can expect from the pageant. Of utmost importance you do not want to start out what could be a wonderful experience by entering a pageant that is not legitimate. Your first step will be to follow the following procedure and try to obtain information before you enter.

When you receive a pageant application, ask questions before you sign on the dotted line.

1) Read through the application thoroughly and have some one close to you read it also.

2) Check the application thoroughly.

3) You will want to know the names of the present and/or former staff members

4) Who will be the emcees

5)   What credentials are required for the panel of judges

6)   Will you need sponsors for the pageant

7)   Who were some of the former contestants and title holder

8)   What prizes, scholarships, contracts, etc are part of the requirements and rewards

9)   Is it a local, national, international, etc.

10)   Where is the pageant being held

For any areas you are unsuccessful in finding the answers, take it a step further and check with the Chamber of Commerce, Department of Tourism, or Department of Economic and Community Development, or write to Pageants Publishing Company World of Beauty Pageants Magazine in Mobile, Alabama and the National Association of Pageant Directors and Judges. Ask them for information concerning this pageant, find out if any complaints have been registered previously, and question them for any pertinent information that they can share with you.

If you cannot find out all the information you need from the pageant director, or any of these sources, then you should consider not entering. Instead, go and see this pageant first and check it out first hand.

If there is a fee to enter, be sure that you not only have the company name, but the name of the individual running the pageant, their address and telephone number. Unless stated otherwise, pay by check or money order so that you have a receipt. If the pageant states it will only accept cash, make sure you get a signed receipt for your money.

Once you are sure of the legitimacy of the pageant, be sure to make a copy of the complete application before putting it in the mail. This way you will have something to refer to as you prepare for entry.

Filling Out The Application

Applications can be very short, or very extensive. No matter which type of application you receive, treat it like you would a job resume. Fill it out completely and have no misspelled words or choppy sentence structure. It will be safer if you make a copy of the application first and try filling it in before completing the original.

The application should be typed, or printed neatly. In many cases, questions asked during an interview will be information taken from your application form so make sure you retain a copy that you can review later. Not only should it be neat so that someone else can read it, but it should contain only information that you think is interesting and that you are able to explain easily during an interview. It should be information that will reflect the type of personality that you wish to project.

For best results, always discuss your application with your sponsor or pageant trainer before submitting it or attempting to fill it out on your own. It is too important to send out haphazardly.

Sponsors/Entry Fees/Ads

It is common for a pageant to require a contestant to pay a sponsor fee or entry fee before being able to participate.

An entry fee is usually a flat fee to cover the cost of processing your application and may go toward the cost of the pageant or toward prizes.

A sponsor fee would be used in similar fashion. You would approach individuals and companies to ask if they are interested in sponsoring you in the pageant. In some cases, pageants give advertising space to a sponsor or offer some incentive. You should know this beforehand.

Advertising space is offered to the contestants, sponsors, individuals or companies to help defray the cost of publishing the pageant program. Any local business can profit from a program advertisement and if you do your homework, you should be able to identify how running an ad will help them. Usually beauty salons, boutiques and small businesses in the beauty or fashion fields will be the strong advertisers and the ones you should consider for sponsorship funds.

In seeking a sponsor, you need to first determine the expenses that you will incur to prepare for the pageant, inclusive of any pageant fees, attire, travel expenses, meals, etc. Once you have an idea of what the total cost to participate will be, you should itemize the expenses and take it with you when you approach a sponsor. In most cases the individual will only ask how the sponsorship will benefit them. You need to be prepared for this question by doing your homework ahead of time. Usually it will result in a free advertisement within the pageant book.

Just like the sponsor weighs the value he will be getting for sponsorship, you also need to be concerned with the benefits you will reap from the pageant. Along with the prizes, you need to consider other aspects such as whether the experience will help you develop your skills further, or other points that you consider to be valuable. It's usually at your discretion to decide if the rewards equal the cost of entering.

Photographs

Any photograph that you are asked to submit should look like you. It should be a professional photo that represents you in your best light and looks like you. In most cases the photograph is returned. Some pageants do not return the photographs that are submitted. You should know this in advance. And, you should also follow the rules for the type of photograph that you are to submit.

Deadlines

Deadlines on pageant entry are set for mailing the applications, advertisements, etc. Don't take them lightly as they are put there for a good reason. Do not wait until the last minute to get your application off in the mail.

When you receive an application for entry, look it over carefully and note the type of information requested. Once you understand all the requirements, start gathering the information you will need in filling out the application. Note the deadlines required to have the details in the pageant director's hands and make sure you send it off at least one week in advance of the deadlines.

If you have not checked the legitimacy of the pageant, you should allow time to do some research before filling in the application and signing on the dotted line. Remember the routine of checking with friends, the local Chamber of Commerce, any individuals you know who have participated in pageants, your pageant trainer or modeling trainer. Don't overlook any avenue that might help in saving you from having a bad experience.

Once you make up your mind to enter, you should fill in the application neatly and thoroughly and double check to make sure you have met all the requirements before you put the stamp on and place it in the mail.

Should You Enter A Pageant

Only you know for sure if you really want to, but maybe some of the following information will help you in understanding if this is something you want to pursue.

Child analysts and experts on children believe that entering small children or teenagers in pageants is mentally healthy. Many mothers will argue against this. My personal feeling is that once a child can comprehend and obtain the valuable lesson of being able to compete with their peers, which they will do all through life in seeking jobs, entering sports, in dance, aerobics, etc. they are old enough to enter a pageant and reap the benefits.

Learning early in life that to lose graciously is to be a winner, or to feel confident enough to compete with your peers can be an extremely, valuable lesson. It will prepare you for the real world. Pageants also seem to help children grow up, face responsibility, and understand the value of learning as much as they can during their school years. This is due to the real fact that pageants do not just judge you on your appearance, but your academic accomplishments as well. If you have less than a "B" average in school, you may find that you will not be qualified to enter most of the pageants that are held throughout the year.

Preparing For A Pageant

Preparation for a pageant will depend on the pageant requirements. Read carefully the dress requirements for your age group and follow them to the letter. In some cases you will only need one outfit, in others you may be required to have a gown or dressy outfit, interview outfit, sportswear, swimsuit, and possibly an additional outfit if you plan to participate in the talent segment.

According to the type of pageant (local, state, national or international) the general layout and requirements will be similar. Check out the pageants and try to develop a critical eye for detail. Don't depend on your memory, write everything down from the length of the pageant, the amount of time you will be on stage, to the lighting used, and the general style of the formal attire as well as the other outfits worn by the contestants. The following list will help you prepare for the day of the pageant.

- Keep photostatic copies of your community service work

- Stay up to date on current events

- Have a dress rehearsal at home before your pageant

- Check over all the clothing to make sure everything is in order

- When packing the clothes, make sure you use tissue paper if the garment is to be folded and have a separate compartment for makeup, jewelry and shoes

- Always carry a spool of thread in each color of your pageant clothes and pins for emergencies.

Pageant Training

Very few contestants win with just basic modeling training. Many make a major mistake by taking the advice of family and friends and not seeking professional advice. A contestant who is really serious about winning should seek pageant training instruction and guidance.

Private training should include sessions covering the applications, photographs, personal appearance, wardrobe, costume, speech, interviews, modeling, swimsuit, talent and judging procedures. Because pageant training is really an individual matter if you want to prepare your maximum potential, you should seek private training sessions. Group lessons accomplish very little.

You should be analyzed to find out your strong points and weak points. You should seek to be as full of vitality at the end of the pageant as you were at the beginning. This will come if you take the training seriously and your trainer is thorough. It isn't an easy, over night course, but an exhausting and time consuming experience. But if it is what you want it can be fun, informative and extremely worthwhile.

The main purpose of a pageant is to select a winner and the purpose of your trainer should be to help you achieve that goal. But there are other benefits that you gain from pageant training.

- You learn how to set goals and to achieve them.

- You discover your assets and learn to work on them.

- You gain poise that can be retained during stress, in front of a camera, on stage, during interviews and talent presentations.

- You learn how to accept constructive criticism.

- You develop your ability to relate to people of all ages, all backgrounds and all styles of living.

- You make lifetime friends as the contestants will have common interests, common goals, and common achievements to begin a foundation of permanent friendship.

- You learn discipline, the pressure of seeking a position, practice public speaking, develop a healthy sense of competition for the future, and learn good sportsmanship.

- Through the constant one on one you learn more about yourself than the average person will learn during a lifetime.

Personal Appearance

As you have heard over and over again, personal appearance is of major importance. Know the image the particular pageant is seeking. Some will emphasize a wholesome and natural look, others prefer a more glamorous look. Once you know this you can prepare yourself accordingly.

If you are at the high or low level of the age group, follow this general rule: Try to look wholesome and youthful for the younger pageant, but older, more sophisticated for the adult competition.

In applying your make up the worse mistakes you can make are:

- Not wear enough color on your lips

- Have your blush not blended on the edges or wear too much blush

- Have your hair in disarray.

A common question asked is what about young children and makeup. In response I would say that make up on small children should be extremely subtle and applied sparingly. The objective is to have the features stand out but not to show that they are enhanced by makeup.

When it comes to photographs, you should have professional photographs made to submit to the pageant. If you prefer a natural look with minimum makeup you will be shocked by the photograph you get. Photography requires more makeup than many people normally wear. When you go to have your pictures done, you will want to wear heavier make up when the photograph is to be black and white and slightly less for color. You should take your make up with you and ask the advice of the photographer as to whether or not you require more or less make up.

As a general guideline you want matte finishes, not frosted makeup. Do use eyeliner and lip pencil. Do use a matte powder to avoid reflection or shine and try to stay away from lip gloss.

What Are Your Chances

If you seek proper training and adhere to the rules, you will rank yourself at the high level of the average contender. According to the law of averages there will be

50% of the competition better than you and 50% will not be as good. Your aim will be to try and pick the five contestants that you feel have the best chance and focus on them. Watch what they do and do your routine, your talent, and your interview better. Aim to be the most poise, and have your physical appearance in tip top shape and you will keep a winning edge.

Stage Fright

It happens to just about everyone. The symptoms of stage fright can range from mild loss of memory to total paralysis. To try, and I say try, to prevent yourself from suffering stage fright, start now to make yourself the center of attention at functions where you have all eyes on you and any chance you get to speak or perform alone on stage, do it. Train yourself to be confident in your ability.

Stage fright comes from the apprehension that you won't be able to remember what you have been trained to do. To avoid this happening practice until you can make every move in your sleep and then try it when awake. Further, if at all possible plan to visit the location of the pageant ahead of time so that you obtain familiarity with the area.

Pageant interviews are exactly like job interviews. When you enter a pageant you are applying for a job. As with a job interview, you would never go into a pageant interview unprepared. In general, know yourself, practice spontaneous questions, tape your voice, learn how to listen carefully and how to interpret questions so that you respond correctly. Whatever you do, never give a cliché answer.

In order to be able to speak on various topics, keep up on current events through reading the paper, watching the news programs on television and thumbing through Newsweek. And, if you find yourself faced with a question that you don't know the answer to say so, but in a proper, intelligent manner. A good example would be to say, "I'm sorry, but no matter how I try, with so many changes happening each day, I'm afraid that I am unprepared for this question." You might even consider throwing in details of activities you participate in that limit the amount of time you have been able to spend on keeping up with current events.

To help you through interviews you can prepare yourself by doing your homework. There are factors that may help you identify the type of questions or at least give you a general idea of what to expect. Look over the following and tips.

- Research the area the pageant is being held in to give you an extra edge.

- Read the judges' bios in the program ahead of time.

- Ask past contestants what questions were asked of them.

Remember, you don't memorize a response, you learn how to respond honestly to the question.

The following will give you an idea of the types of questions that are usually asked during interviews for pageants. Look over the list and try and determine what you would answer.

Typical Interview Questions

- Do you have a hobby? If so, what is your hobby?

- What is your favorite sport?

- What is your favorite TV show and why do you like it?

- Do you have a favorite story you have read? What is the title of the story?

- Who is your favorite actress?

- Who is your favorite actor?

- Who is your favorite recording star and why?

- If you should win the stile, what do you think will be expected of you?

- Explain to the judges, how you go about making friends.

- When you are introduced to a grown up, what do you say to them?

- What is the worse thing that ever happened to you?

- What is the best thing that ever happened to you?

- If someone says that you're pretty or cute, how do you respond?

- What do you think about yourself?

- What do you think about your best friend?

- What do you think about your family?

- Would you consider yourself a tomboy, or a young lady in the way you act and why?

- What interest you most in life?

- What do you dislike most in life?

- If you could go anywhere in the world, where would you go and why?

- Do you like doing things by yourself or prefer doing something with someone else?

- Do you like yourself? What do you consider to be your best quality as a person?

- What do you like most about yourself and why?

- If you could have one wish, what would you wish and why?

- Who are the most important people in your life and why do you consider them to be important?

- What do you think about school?

- Please describe to the judges how an average school day goes for you.

- Do you like your teachers. Do you have a favorite teacher?

- Do you consider yourself as acting your age or acting older and why?

- If you were asked to make a choice between the following three things, what would you choose and why:?   a) new dress, b) candy, c) money.

- What is your favorite color. What colors do you like to wear with this color?

- Describe what being "you" means?

- What is your favorite book to read and how would you classify it?

- What is your favorite food, and what is your favorite meal?

- How tall would you like to be and why?

- Describe your mother and your father as they appear to you?

- What do you think about boys? Do you think they make good friends?

- Do you like to play with dolls? If so do you play with them often or only once in a while?

- Do you like to play with guns or trucks? If so, why? If not, why not?

- Do you and your family do fun things together? How does doing these things with your family make you feel?

- Who in your family do you think you are most like and why?

- Do people like you when they first meet you, or do you have to work at making people like you. Why do you think this is so?

- Do you act one way with adults, a different way with peers, and different with your family, or do you always act the same.

- Do you plan on continuing in pageants, why?

- Have you make many new friends at pageants? If so, do you see them only at pageants or at other times?

- How old are you? What does being your age mean to you?

- Did you want to enter this pageant or did someone encourage you to?

- How many pageants have you entered and what do you think you have gotten out of them?

- Describe to the judges what you will do if you don't win in this pageant?

- Do your friends treat you any different now then they did before you started entering pageants? If so, describe how they act differently?

- What do you want to be when you grow up and why?

- What's your favorite subject in school and why do you like this subject?

- Who is your best friend and why do you consider this person to be your best friend?

- If you were asked to describe yourself to someone over the phone, what would you say?

- Do you worry what your family thinks about your involvement in a pageant? Do you ever wonder how they feel when you don't win?

- What is your most favorite thing in the world and why?

- If you could be any age, how old would you be and why?

- If you were given a choice between a wish for yourself, or for your family, who would you make the wish for and what would that wish be?

- If you asked to do something that meant a lot to you and you are told "no" what do you do?

- If you could change one thing about your school, what would it be?

- What is your definition of a winner?

- If you had a chance to get one message across to your listeners, what subject would it be on?

- What have you personally learned about preparing for pageants?

- If you could change one thing in the country, what would you change?

- Do you believe there is a generation gap? What do you feel is the biggest problem between parents and children today?

- If you could tell me only one thing about yourself, what would you tell me?

- In your estimation, what makes a good leader?

- What is the most pressing problem facing young people today?

- If you could add a course to your school's present curriculum, what would it be and why?

- Do you feel it is important to be a goal setter? Why or why not?

- Do you consider it to be more important to be liked or to be respected. Why?

- If you had to rate your appearance, your personality and your achievements from 1 to 10, what would your score be?

- If your career plans did not work out, what would you do?

- Tell me your biggest fantasy?

- How would you like to broaden yourself as a person?

- What do you hope to be doing five years from now? What three people in history do you admire and why?

- What century other than the present would you like to live in?

- What are your plans for the future?

- What is your weakest point?

- Do you feel that the best time in your life has passed, is happening now, or is coming in the future, and why?

- Give three words that describes you best.

- What motivates you and why?

- If you had one million dollars to spend, what would you do with it?

In Conclusion

To help you in preparing for pageants, the following will give you a little more advice to help you on your way to being a winner.

Talent Competitions

Don't shy away from entering the talent segment of the pageant. Talent competitions can cover a realm of artistic areas. You can enter a talent segment to sing, dance, do a monologue, read poetry, lipsync, do gymnastics, baton twirl, play a musical instrument, etc. The judging areas will be just as versatile from the execution, the skill level, the interpretation, originality, costume, props, time limit, potential, entertainment value, etc.

It goes without saying that you should prepare yourself and what you plan to do for your talent. If it is dancing, you should take lessons. If you wish to sing, you should find a singing instructor to help you perfect your performance. Don't just select something to do and then not follow through in the preparation.

Attire

When it comes to interpreting the formal wear, this is where the worse mistakes crop up. A word to the wise, dresses for children should be short and reach the tips of the child's fingers. Don't make the dress so full that the child cannot hold her arms near her sides. For evening gowns do not choose one that is too fussy and make sure that for a teenager it is not slinky, or a tight sequin gown, or a hoop skirt. Hoop skirts should be worn by contestants up to the teenage level and no further. The most appealing style would be for the early teen to wear a full or A line skirt made of chiffon or any soft fabric. For mid teens and up to eighteen a full, A line or straight skirt, with beads, sequins, etc. on the bodice. For ages above eighteen there is no general rule except keep it simple the key to chic. You will find that form fitting gowns will add height and sophistication, strapless gowns are a nice change from the trend as well.

To make yourself stand out, have a gimmick during the competition that makes you stand out from the crowd. This can be carrying the same color through in each item of attire you will wear on stage, or the same style of neckline on each piece of attire, or a conversation piece that you wear with each piece of attire.

Pageants can be exciting for you and for your family. It is the well rounded girl who walks away the winner and not the one who is the most beautiful. Looks play a role, but the role for winning is based on how well you do with what you have. The contestant who has perfected their appearance, attitude and the way they carry themselves will be the winner.

Pageants are good for you and will help motivate you toward becoming the best you can possibly be. You will gain confidence, experience, and get to know yourself better. Don't cheat yourself of a chance of a life time.

Pageant Listing

If you are still determined that you wish to participate in pageants, the following listing will give you some ideas of pageants that are run. It is impossible to give you a complete list, but the information you have gathered in this section will help you in locating others. This is just a starting point and you may find that these pageants are non-existent in your area. Some of the pertinent information is printed here to help you contact the pageant if it seems to be one you are interested in. Because pageants change their requirements and entry fees, you should call to verify the current details for the pageant. You may also find that the pageants are no longer in existence. So keeping all this in mind, look over the information, go to the websites for up-to-date information and re-verify each time you plan to enter.

- www.teenagerpageants.com
- www.GalaxyPageants.com
- www.sunburstbeauty.com/
- www.foreverbeautifulpageants.com/

Preparation

Your first step will be to decide on the type and size of the company you wish to work for. Determine if you wish to work for a manufacturing industry, a service industry, a government agency, or an educational institution. Check into the various companies in your area to help you make the selection.

The Big Four Pageants

Once you have experienced a pageant, you might want to consider the most popular pageants for older teens and adults. The four major international beauty pageants for women – Miss World, Miss Universe, Miss International and Miss Earth.

- Miss World is the oldest existing major international beauty pageant. It was created by Eric Morley in 1951 and since his death, Morley's wife, Julia Morley, co-chairs the pageant

- Miss Universe is an annual international beauty contest that is run by the Miss Universe Organization.

- Miss International, also called "Miss International Beauty". The contestants are expected to serve as "Ambassadors of Peace and Beauty", showing tenderness, benevolence, friendship, beauty, intelligence, ability to take action, and great international sensibility. The ultimate goal of the Miss International beauty pageant is to promote world peace, goodwill, and understanding.

- Miss Earth is an annual pageant organised by Philippine-based Carousel Productions through the Miss Earth FoundationThe non-profit organization aims to promote awareness levels and knowledge on current environmental issues and what actions can be done by power of broadcasting and other media campaigns globally where the annual winners are expected to spend a year delivering talks to schools and other organizations and work on projects with other institutions, including Greenpeace, World Wildlife Foundation, and United Nations Environment Program.

LESSON 24:
THE WORLD OF BUSINESS

We start developing a group of skills early in life. If this were not true, as babies, we would not have been able to make our parents aware of our needs. Though primitive methods are employed at birth, they still help us to communicate with the world around us.

We continue to develop and start to refine our communication skills. At first we learn facial expressions, body movements, speech patterns, and, of course, language. This learning process is continual. Eventually we master the art of communication and go on to learn about the world around us. That's where the fascination begins as we start becoming part of the world around us. But this doesn't happen for everyone! For some the skill of communicating becomes a continual quest that they somehow can't seem to master.

Much later in our developmental process we develop the skill of "reading" reactions. This skill grows until we learn to not blurt out the first thought in our minds and become more selective in vocabulary and speech patterns. In some instances this may present pauses in our speech. That is acceptable if the pause is brief and you are able to find suitable words quickly. When we have a limited vocabulary, the pause lengthens and the context of our conversation becomes lost and we find people tend not to listen to what we are saying.

Even those with extensive vocabularies, however, experience doubts in unfamiliar situations. But an extensive vocabulary will never put you in a situation of being misunderstood in a business situation. How important is it to increase our vocabulary? In the world of business this can not only be costly but can lead to embarrassment. You need to learn how to communicate effectively if you plan on entering the world of business.

So how do you go about improving your vocabulary? You do it by learning new words and practicing them in your everyday speech. Starting now you should begin to read extensively (magazines, newspapers, books, business journals, etc.) You should look up any words that you hear for the first time and try putting them into sentences so that you can add them to your vocabulary. You need to find a method of exposing yourself to new words every day. You can pick up words even when watching television, or if you have the interest, doing crossword puzzles and word games will help to increase the words you are able to use when communicating.

Another important facet of communication is being able to understand the "lingo". You need to be able to use the proper words to describe situations within the business world. For instance, if you are conversing about computers, don't say that "thingamajig". Instead learn the proper name for the parts of the computer. This is true with every aspect of business. Once you know what field you want to enter, remember that the "lingo" needs to be learned as well as the skills and techniques.

When you are well-versed on a subject you can communicate properly. You will find that you can add to conversations and feel comfortable that what you say is not only understood, but spoken in a professional way. Professionalism comes once you have your act together.

This will take some time, but if you start now to work on your vocabulary and expand it thoroughly in the area of business you enter, you have supplied yourself with a very important tool in the business world. The art of communication will take you to the limits!

If it were necessary to describe what is happening in the business world in one word, the word would be computers We live in an age of computers. Between now and the year 2000, the biggest change in the business world, as well as in our personal lives, will be a result of the electronic industry. Experts are claiming that the world is on the threshold of a computer revolution. Don't shy away from it, it is a necessity for you to become more and more familiar with computers if you hope to succeed in business. Just like the typewriter, once a necessary piece of equipment in all offices and now almost extinct, you will be too if you don't keep up with the changes.

To prepare yourself for the marketplace, you should check into classes being offered in computer training. Most schools, colleges and universities offer such training during the day and in the evening. The type of courses you should include the following:

- Computer Concept or Computer Literacy Course

- Windows Course

- Word Processing Course (Word or WordPerfect seem to be in demand these days.)

- Spreadsheet Course (Excel and Lotus are most popular.)

- Database Course (Access and Dbase are the forerunners.)

Additionally you might consider desktop publishing and a business graphics program. In all cases you should seek training on the latest versions of the programs if you are not preparing for a specific job request. You can easily find out what version is currently out by doing some reasearch at a library or checking around with people you know who are familiar with computers and current versions of programs. Another way of handling this would be by checking in book stores or even calling program manufacturers. Usually you will find their numbers in books on how to use the programs.

Just as important will be to have a resource book that you will be able to review or later keep at your desk once you land a job. If you learn a program you don't want to forget how to operate it and if you don't have access to a computer to practice, you may lose the skills you learned.

Another change that has been surfacing is the increased use of contract workers. Contract workers are hired by a company through a placement agency. The terms of any given assignment may vary, with some going on to permanent hiring. Don't think of this as a reflection on your ability as it is a method put in place by businesses to meet the changes in the environment. Contractors are hired at a set rate and there are no benefits provided by the business where they are placed. The dollar amount being saved in this transaction is becoming more appealing as the responsibilities for the individual rests with the contracting firm. In some organizations total dependency for getting new employees as well as contractors is in the hands of contracting agencies. Using this method allows the company a chance to "try out" the employee before making any hiring decision. So in setting up your job search method, do not exclude responding to ads by contracting companies for positions they have open.

Education is essential. You need to keep abreast of changes, or fit into the modernized business world of working quickly and efficiently. From the lowest point on the corporate ladder, up to and including the top rung, you will need competencies in English, Spelling, Math. You will need to develop accuracy and quickness in performing tasks. You will need knowledge on sources to reference for informational purposes. Skills in both oral and written communication will need to be perfectly polished. To this you will need to develop your skills in human relations and decision making.

But developing skills and using them is not enough. In order to be a success you must be able to accept yourself. Some of the most miserable people in the world are those who continually strive to be something they are not. You need to trust yourself. When you trust yourself your special traits come to the surface and you are aware of how much you have to offer as an individual.

Trusting and knowing who you are is not enough either. You must be genuine, open to experience, and accepting of others. If you lack in this area you will fail. Think of a failure as a person who is uncertain about themselves and others, who is lonely as a result of trying to protect themselves against being hurt, and who is insecure as a result of feelings of inadequacy. No one wants to find themselves in this predicament and it doesn't have to be so. Start now to try and improve in the areas where you lack development and you will meet with success. Once you understand your tailoring for the business world, you can better understand the needs of others in the company. If you are to become part of the business world, you will be part of a family, and that family will be the company.

A company is an organization with needs. It is a collection of individuals each with their own needs and wants. The company's needs consist of such things as producing a product or service, making a profit, and growing and expanding. The individual needs of employees are met by such things as making enough money to provide an acceptable standard of living, satisfying social needs by being a part of a company's family, and satisfying esteem needs by having a job that is important. So are you equipped to fit into the business world? You are the only one who can answer that answer. You will need the basic skills.

Communication Skills

Once you have obtained the proper education to do a specific job, increased your vocabulary skills and put in place a method of keeping up with the world around you. You need to concentrate on learning how to communicate. Communication is a major part of human relations. On any job it is essential that you communicate with your employer, your fellow workers, and people outside the company. It is a two way process in which information is accurately received and understood in order that some action can be taken. To be an effective communicator you should listen with openness, be sensitive to the receiver's world, use direct, simple language, utilize any feedback, repeat when necessary and think before you speak.

Listening Skills

Listening is just as important as communication. Studies show that the average person spends 70 percent of his or her day communicating; 45 percent of that communication time is spent listening. Hearing does not automatically imply listening. A person can hear sounds that come from another person and not understand the words. Listening is the complete process of oral language, communicated by a source, received, recognized, reacted to, comprehended, and retained.

If you have recognized problems in your communicating or listening abilities, start now to practice proper listening and communicating skills. Remember that it not only saves time, but shows professionalism if you ask for clarification, and present input at the point of the initial communication. It is poor business etiquette to wait or do something wrong. It is better to express any misunderstandings and obtain an impressive conclusion.

Selecting Your Position

Once you are ready to enter the business world you need to consider the type of position you want and the type of company you wish to work for. Next you need to find out job availability and then prepare the tools necessary to obtain the position. Remember that you need to convince the interviewer that you have the skills and that you are the right person for the job.

Career Goals

Next you should establish your career goals. How long do you plan to work. Set a timetable for where you expect to be in the company after one year, five years, ten years, etc. If you wish to move up in a company choose a company with career opportunities to meet your goals.

You need to decide if you wish to work for a small company or a large company. Speak to individuals, counselors, teachers, etc. about the advantages and disadvantages with both sizes. Take the feedback and make your decision.

Start reading the want ads in the newspapers, register with State employment agencies, visit private employment agencies, watch for Civil Service announcements. All of this you will do while you prepare for your initial contact with the companies that interest you. Once you have made a decision, it's time to go into action.

Writing A Letter Of Application

The letter of application is often the key to securing an interesting and challenging position that will give you economic security. It is the cover letter that provides an introduction to you and your accomplishments. Usually the cover letter will be sent with your resume.

The cover letter may be the most important letter you will ever write. It is basically a sales letter as it shows your services, skills, knowledge, and abilities to the employer. The letter should arouse interest, describe your abilities and request an interview.

Techniques

The letter must be neat and well thought out if it is to be impressive. You should read the letter carefully for any spelling or grammatical errors and address it to a specific person in a proper letter style.

Use the "you" approach. This means that the writing is done from the reader's point of view. You want to discuss what you can do for the company, but from the perspective of what the company needs. Let the reader know that you understand the requirements of the position and that you have the qualifications and willingness necessary to do a good job for the company. Be honest and tell the reader what you can do, but do not exaggerate. After all, if you get the job, you will be expected to perform in the areas that you specified.

To help you develop a good cover letter, look over the following details and do not omit one from your finished product.

- Address it to someone in authority who is responsible for making decisions on hiring. You should use their name and title, but if it is impossible to get that information, use a functional title such as "Dear Manager".

- Tell how you learned about this particular company.

- Demonstrate the knowledge you have gathered on the company and something that will let them know you are aware of their current problems, interests and priorities.

- Convey your interest and let them know that you are committed to doing a good job.

- Be friendly and personal, yet balance this with professionalism. Only share information that is pertinent to the position.

- Try to think of something that sets you out from others who will be applying for the job. If you've done your homework you should be able to pick something relevant that gives you an "edge".

- Be direct in specifying the position you are applying for and hope to obtain.

- Be brief and focused on the objective. You can cover a lot of territory with few words if they are well chosen.

I'm sure you are wondering how to cover all this territory in a short cover letter. Take a look at the advertisement and the cover letter that follows. This will give you an idea of how to go about preparing your cover letter.

In looking over the cover letter, refer back to the advertisement and try to ascertain how you should approach an ad that covers your job qualifications and the position that you are applying for. It becomes very important to make sure that not only your cover letter is designed to respond to the advertisement, but your resume as well. If you have a resume that you have been using for all the positions you apply for, it's time to realize that not only will you need to tailor the cover letter, but the resume as well. We will be covering the resume a little later in this lesson.

As you read over the cover letter, notice how it relates back to the advertisement, covering the pertinent points and giving only the information that is needed to identify the individual, present the skills, and clearly state the position. Several points were highlighted that will make this individual stand out from the rest, which is what your aim should be.

COMPUTER SUPPORT/HELPDESK
OPERATIONS: Help desk administration support for PC
computer systems. 1-5 years exp. providing on-line phone
problem resolution services is required w/exposure to
WINDOWS, WORD, EXCEL software in WINDOWS
environment. Configuration skills desired. Customer
service skills are essential. Send resume to Beth Schuller,
Computer Integrity, 640 Kreag Road, Rochester, NY
14634.

The Cover Letter

COVER LETTER

JENNIFER PETERS
991 SOUTH AVENUE
ROCHESTER NY 14626

October 12, 2916

Beth Schuller
Computer Integrity
 640 Kreag Road
Rochester, NY 14634

Dear Ms. Schuller:

RE: COMPUTER SUPPORT/HELPDESK OPERATIONS:

I was very pleased to learn of the opening for the position of computer support person for a NOVELL network with MS/DOS systems.

On my enclosed resume I have outlined my professional experience that extends a period of 10 years. I also have obtained by BA in computer science that has prepared me for a job such as the one you are offering. My resume has been tailored to the experiences and accomplishments that address the requirements for this position.

I am a "take charge" type of person and have demonstrated strong leadership skills when presented with a difficult situation. I have a strong record of success in troubleshooting problems with PC's and NOVELL networks.

It is my nature and philosophy to always try and help and do whatever is necessary to get the job done. I recently obtained my CNA so that I could better service customers who are experiencing problems with their equipment.

I would welcome the opportunity to share with you additional examples of my contribution to organizations such as your own. I would appreciate a personal interview with you to discuss my application further.

Sincerely,

Jennifer Peters

The Resume

Just as important as the letter of application is the resume. A resume is intended to relieve the application letter of many details regarding your qualifications. It provides a summary of your education and experience. Just as the letter of application is a sales letter, so the resume is a piece of sales literature. It represents a very important product YOU.

Prior to the anti discrimination legislation of the 1960s and 70s, almost all resumes had a section labeled "Personal Data." This section included such things as age, marital status, number of children, height, weight, and hobbies. Our laws now state that it is illegal to discriminate on the basis of age, race, sex, etc. Therefore, leave the personal items off your resume. The employer needs to have the information to make a decision on whether you have the qualifications for the job.

In developing a good resume, refer to the following points:

- A good resume is lean and to the point.
- It is also straight forward and honest.
- You should discourage going into detailed descriptions and leave out the words, "responsibilities include".

- When putting in the dates for education or employment, just include the years, not the month and day.
- A resume should be designed to get the job interview initially, and then the job, so treat it like a marketing tool that is presenting YOU as the product.

- It should be neatly typed and reproduced on any standard resume paper, but stick with an off-white, light beige, or while shade.

There are many books on the market that will help you in laying out the design and content of your resume. Here we will review the sections and then present a sample of a resume that is geared toward meeting the objectives of a job offering. I strongly suggest that you either purchase or make a trip to the library to look over other examples in resume and cover letter books. One that I would recommend is called, "The Damn Good Resume Guide", by Yana Parker. This book provides a discussion on the parts of the cover letter and resume. It follows up with examples of both geared toward various employment positions.

Sections Of The Resume

- A clearly stated career objective should be the first section on the resume. You should present a short sentence that states precisely the position you seek and any long range career goals.

- A summary of your qualifications should be highlighted after your career objective. It should be stated in concise sentences and only include relevant details.

- A chronological work history should follow. This should be inclusive of all experience that pertains to the position.

- Finally a listing of relevant education and training should appear.

That is what the resume should contain. The following is an example that you can refer to when you set up your resume.

OBJECTIVE: Position as a system and software technician

HIGHLIGHTS OF QUALIFICATIONS

- Over 10 years' experience in software training and system support services
- Extensive knowledge on MS/DOS (inclusive of Version 6.2), Windows 3.1, Word, Excel, Lotus & WordPerfect (up to and including the current versions of the software)
- Professional training in troubleshooting, repairing, and configuring Novell Network systems
- Published technical author and editor in the field of computer software
- Enjoy working as a team and interacting with individuals to help solve their problems
- Read extensively in computer systems, peripherals, and software to keep up with the current versions and models on the market

RELEVANT EXPERIENCE & ACCOMPLISHMENTS

Computer Systems
- Worked as a system support technician for IBM and Rochester Tel through a local temporary agency. Provided telephone support to company employees experiencing LAN, NOVELL, or PC based problems
- Researched and developed a technical manual describing the procedures and questions to use in identifying system problems, including step by step instructions on solving the most frequent situations coming into the support system group.
- Did extensive studying and passed the CNA exam to provide the best possible system support to the clients.
- Worked part time as an instructor at Bryant & Stratton for PC Concepts course.

Software
- Instructor for Bryant & Stratton for computer software programs including Word, WordPerfect Lotus, Excel, DOS and Windows. Proficient on many versions of the programs
- Perform system setups and software training to individuals and companies as part of a small company I formed in 1984

EMPLOYMENT HISTORY

1994 - present	Software Instructor, Bryant & Stratton, Rochester, NY
1990 - 1993	Help Desk Technician, Rochester Tel, Rochester, NY
1990 - 1993	Software Instructor, Bryant & Stratton, Rochester, NY

1987 - 1993	Help Desk Technician, IBM, Rochester, NY
1987 - 1993	Software Instructor, Bryant & Stratton, Rochester, NY
1984 - 1987	System Documenter/Project Coordinator, Eastman Kodak, Rochester, NY

EDUCATION & TRAINING

A.A. Degree in Business - Monroe Community College, Rochester, 1984-86
B.A. Degree in Computer Science - Rochester Institute of Technology, Rochester, 1987-1993
CNA Degree - Institute for System Support, Berkeley, 1994
Certificates of Completion PC & Macintosh Systems - Logical Operations, Rochester, 1990-92
Certificates of Completion WordPerfect, Word, Lotus & Excel - Logical Operation, 1990-94

The Initial Interview

The interview will not be an ordeal if you adequately prepare for it. Knowledge of what to do and what to say will help eliminate a great deal of nervousness. If you use some of the techniques described in this book, your poise and assurance will greatly improve. Remember that you are striving to sell skills and knowledge that are needed by the company. Consider the interview as a "sizing up" process an opportunity to get acquainted with someone and you will gain confidence.

First impressions are important so check your personal appearance making sure you have utilized all that you have learned. Take time to think about the questions that you may be asked and work on responses so that you speak in a firm, clear voice and give direct answers. Make sure that you take what you may need with you. You should have a pen, a small notebook, a pocket dictionary, an extra copy of your resume and any pertinent data that may aid in landing the position (grade transcripts, letter of recommendations, special awards or certificates, etc.)

Questions that are common asked in an interview are:

- "Why do you wish to work for this company?"
- "What salary do you expect to receive?"

- "Where have you worked previously?"
- "What skills do you have that will help you do this job?"
- "Do you have any questions?"

If you are asked to fill out a job application you will need your resume, social security number, addresses and telephone numbers of references and companies. Be sure you have this information with you.

There has been a lot of talk recently abut "behavioral interviewing", especial in high-tech and accounting organizations. Behavior-based interviewing is designed to end "snap judgments" in the hiring process. Snap, or gut feeling interviews are based on subjective impressions rather than objective information. When approaching an interview from this ankle, the basis becomes more a stereotyping rather than an assessment of the candidate.

In some cases the traditional approach has been to select a candidate by what could be termed, "trait interviewing". This type of interview attempts to match a candidate's traits to those required to do a job successfully. If for instance "dependable" is a job requirement, the person handling the interview will attempt to gauge this characteristic in the candidates. The problem is that the trait becomes more a label that ends up reflecting an impression rather than information.

All of these problems in the standard ways of handling an interview has lead to using behavior-based interviewing. It is structured so that every candidate is given the same general questions which results in examples of behavior instead of a collection of statements. This data is used as a base line for future interviews. Current employees' responses and their actual behavior provides a guideline for use in evaluating future hires.

If you are confronted with a behavior-based interview you will find that the skills needed to do the job are defined and codified into two categories.

TECHNICAL SKILLS: Skills normally obtained through formal education or hands-on experience.

PERFORMANCE SKILLS: More like habits that can determine how a person will perform on the job. Examples would be decisiveness or creativity.

You can also assume that you will be required to give concrete examples of how your past performance supports your stated skills. You can also expect to be asked for specific examples of dependability.

You can see why this type of interviewing is becoming popular. Past achievements are a direct measure for future achievements. Even though people continue to learn and grow, their past behavior is still the best indicator of their future behavior.

Technical skills are the specific knowledge and hands-on skills required and are typically learned in a formal educational environment

Getting The Job

Once you are notified that you have landed the job, you have work to do. You know that the job meets your objectives or you would not have gone on the interview. But there are certain things that you now need to find out. Make sure that you have these questions answered and that you understand what is expected of you.

Questions To Ask

- When do I begin working?
- To whom should I report?
- What are the working hours?
- What is the company dress code?

You will need to obtain information on the company you will be working for so that you can see how your position fits into the overall picture. A little history on the company can also be beneficial. Of utmost important you need to be aware of the formal (written) and informal (understood) company policies. You should obtain a copy of the policies and procedures manual for the company which will spell out working hours, pay raises, evaluation procedures, vacation periods, sick leave, insurance benefits, retirement benefits, termination policies, etc.

Business Etiquette

Business and social etiquette are very similar. Business etiquette differs from social as it is based on the system of rank and position, while social considers everyone equal. No matter how capable you are, you can lose the job if you do not employ business etiquette at your initial contact, and later on the job.

Conduct With Management

A loose tongue, sinks ships. You can be a valued employee, but may find yourself on your way out the door if you do not learn what to say and how to say it in the office environment. The following will help you keep the position once you have made it in the door.

- Address superior officers by their title even if they call you by your first name. In the presence of outsiders or clients, also address your co workers by their title.
- Avoid discussing business matters outside business. Be loyal to your place of business and to your boss.
- Pay particular attention to the channels of authority and do not go over someone's head at any time.
- Do not criticize superiors or anyone else for that matter.
- Show courtesy to your superiors.
- Learn the company rules and regulations as quickly as possible and then adhere to them.
- Be on time and do not stop before the close of the day.
- Limit your personal telephone calls to those that are absolutely necessary and keep the conversation to the absolute minimum. It will be best to make these calls during your lunch period if possible.

Conduct With Co Workers

In a business office be businesslike. How many times have you heard this clique? It still is true today. Look over the following pointers to help you formulate a proper conduct with co-workers.

- Do not discuss private affairs. Do not gossip, laugh loudly, joke, or carry on endless conversations. You were hired to work, not have a social club.

- Respect the work and property of others. Be neat and efficient and well organized at all times.

- Refrain from establishing fast friendships in business especially during the early part of your employment. In lunching with co workers do not discuss the boss, the business, or criticize others in the company.

- Be politely reserved in all your business relations and most certainly curb your temper. Emotional outbursts and loud speech are the epitome of bad manners at any time or any place.

- Never forget the everyday courtesy of "please" and "thank you".

- Keep the Ladies' room neat. Just remember the old saying, "What, where you brought up in a barn."

Telephone Etiquette

What is considered to be good telephone etiquette? As a general guide, the following will help you in developing your telephone skills:

- Be sure your voice tone is pleasant, cordial and sincere.

- Speak clearly and distinctly into the receive so you can be heard and understood.

- Identify yourself both in answering the telephone and in making calls. Also identify the company and your superior or department, whichever the company policy calls for.

- Take messages properly. Politely request the caller's name, number, or other information when the person for whom the call is intended is out of the office.

- Make sure your are aware of how the office phone is to be answered, the policy concerning incoming calls and the information you should obtain.

- Make your conversation brief and end your conversation courteously. Wait for the other person to say goodbye, then hang up the receiver gently.

Putting It Into Practice

The following section is geared toward a position of a secretary or receptionist but today with the "trimming" of the work force becomes useful in most office positions. Even as the manager of the department, you may on occasion have to answer a phone and take a message. The following will be helpful to everyone who works with a group of people and is in the habit of answering a ringing phone.

<u>Helping The Manager In Handling Callers</u>

The executive will rarely tell you what he or she expects of you in your role as receptionist. You need to know the general instructions:

- Find out the name of the caller, company affiliation, and the purpose of their call or visit to the office. Try to remember the names and faces of frequent callers or visitors so you can greet them more cordially.

- Maintain the good will of the person by making their contact with the firm both pleasant and satisfactory. Try to make the caller or visitor feel comfortable while waiting to see the manager.

- Judge which callers the manager will welcome, which he or she wants to avoid, which should be seen by someone else in the company, and which you should handle yourself.

- Make explanations to those callers whom the manager will not see. This should be done without antagonizing the caller.

Receiving Callers

Organizations have their own methods of receiving a caller. In most large organizations the caller is received in a reception area where a trained receptionist will take care of the preliminaries and advise the secretary that the caller has arrived.

The secretary will go to the reception area and escort the visitor to the manager's office. The secretary should introduce herself to the caller, using his or her name and ask them to come with her to the office. (Example: "Mr. Peters? I'm Mr Johnson's secretary. Will you come with me, please?")

The secretary should not attempt to carry on a conversation with the caller, but should respond cordially to any remarks or questions.

Greeting A Caller

Formality is appropriate in greeting an office caller. (Example: "How do you do?" "Good morning." You should not offer your hand. Let the caller make the first gesture toward shaking hands. If your desk is at the entrance of the office, you need not rise to speak to a caller. If the caller does not volunteer any information, you should smile and ask, "May I help you?"

Never say, "Hello."

Determining The Purpose Of A Call

A secretary is usually expected to ask why a caller wants to see the manager. This should be done whether the caller comes to the office or is on the telephone. Make sure you use a pleasant voice with a smile when trying to get information. Use tact, discretion and patience. (Example: "Good morning, Mr. Peters. I'm Mr. Jones' secretary. He's busy at the moment, but is there anything I can do for you?" or change the last part to "What can I do for you?", "Can I be of any help to you?")

If the caller states his purpose you can either schedule an appointment, check with the manager for further instructions, or ask the caller to leave his card and you will get back to him when you have a chance to talk with Mr. Jones.

If you have been instructed to find out the purpose of each caller, what do you do if they say it is personal?

(Example: "I'm sorry, Mr. Peters, but Mr. Jones has informed me to ask all callers before scheduling an appointment. Could you give me a general idea?" or "So that I do not waste your time, I must follow our office policy in announcing a caller, or scheduling an appointment. I cannot inform Mr. Jones of your call unless I have this information." or "In that case, Mr. Peters, perhaps you could write Mr. Jones a letter and tell him briefly what you wish to see him about and ask for an appointment. Then he will be able to make his own decision."

Making A Caller Comfortable

Show a caller who is to see your employer where to leave his or her hat, coat, briefcase and any other articles that he or she will not require for the appointment. Offer to take care of the items for the caller. Offer the caller a seat, newspaper or magazine to make them comfortable. Ask if there is anything you can get for them, or anyway you can be of help while they wait.

Do not begin a conversation with a caller unless they show an inclination to talk. This is where your communication skills will come into play. Talk on topics of interest to the caller, but avoid controversial issues. If the caller asks about the company, reply only in generalities.

How To Announce A Caller

If the caller is known to the manager or has visited the office before you can say, "Mr. Johnson is free now. Won't you go right in?" If the caller is making his first visit to the office or is an infrequent caller you should accompany him to the door of the manager's office, step to one side and say, "Mr. Johnson, Mr. Smith" or "Mr. Johnson, this is Mr. Smith."

A Caller The Manager Does Not Want To See

Use tact in dealing with a caller who the manager will not see. (Example: Mr. Knight, Ms. Evans is concerned with some emergencies and will be for some time. I wish I could be more helpful to you, but may I suggest that you take your matter up with her in writing for the time being."

A Caller Who You Need To Refer To Another Person In The Company

When you find that the purpose of a caller's visit involves a matter that should be taken up with someone else in the company, if you handle the matter properly, the caller will thank you for saving his time. If you do not, the caller will take offense. (Example: "Mr. Brown, this is a matter that Mr. Jones would have Mr. Peters handle. Mr. Peters is our account executive and is better able to help you. I'll be glad to make an appoint for you with Mr. Peters." or "Would you like me to call Mr. Peters now and see if he is available?"

Calls By Office Personnel

If the company has an open door policy, the secretary does not inquire about the purpose of the appointment with the manager when the caller is a company person. It may be advisable when a new or young employee asks to see the manager to ask if you might be of any help. In this way you may save the manager valuable time in dealing with every problem that comes up. You may inform the employee that you can save them the problem of waiting for an appointment if they will tell you the problem. In this way you can offer some suggestions or help them in adhering to company policy in dealing with complaints. If the employee does not want to confide in you, do not urge him to, but instead give the manager a note of who is waiting to see him.

Interrupting Conferences

Try to avoid interrupting a conference, but if it is essential, type on a slip of paper any message that must be delivered to someone in the conference room. If you require instructions to handle the matter, put the questions on the paper that you hand to the individual and wait for instructions.

Telephone Calls For A Caller

Ask the person calling if it is possible for you to take the message. If the person insists on speaking with the visitor, enter the conference room, apologize for the interruption to all present, and address the individual who has the call. Ask if they would like to take the call in the conference room or at your desk.

Be prepared for them asking you to take a message. In this case inform the called politely that the individual is in the middle of an important matter and would like to have the opportunity of calling them back.

Helping A New Employee

A new secretary or any new employee appreciates it when co workers give them a friendly reception and help familiarize them with the company. Assisting in work production and methods of production will help the individual become proficient and not dependable in the long run.

Make sure that a newcomer is introduced to co workers so that they are aware of the individuals and their positions in the company.

If you are the newcomer, do not discuss your old company policies or procedures. Once you are established you might present these as suggestions if you feel that they may help the company.

Use Of First Names

Most modern offices are informal and use the first names among employees. The basic rule is that you may follow the practice that has been established in your particular office. If the policy is first names, your supervisor must give his or her permission personally for you to use their first name. When there are visitors present, you should address your supervisor with Mr., Ms, etc.

If you follow these guidelines, incorporate standard etiquette policies, you will find that you are accepted and respected in your position.

The Grapevine Of Gossip

A grapevine is a trail of office gossip passed from one employee to another by word of mouth. The smart office person regards any grapevine news with caution. Never spread rumors and keep in mind that a rumor can have serious consequences when it gets outside the company. Don't participate in hurting yourself, others, or the company as a whole.

Further Guidelines

As a general rule to avoid conflict within or outside the company, adhere to the following:

- If a co worker is having small talk with you and a client enters the area, try to draw the conversation to a close gracefully, or say, "Excuse me....."
- If a fellow employee is not appropriately dressed, it is not your place to say anything, unless you are asked. This is a matter for their supervisor to discuss.
- If you find an error in a report that the manager has given you to type you should correct it and not

make reference to it. If it represents a major change and affects the results of the report, you should show the manager your change and ask if he would mind checking it for you.

- If you are reprimanded for not getting a report or letter to the manager on time, or if he or she discovers an error. whether the fault is solely yours or not, apologize to the manager and then tactfully bring the matter to the other individual's attention so that they can avoid this happening again.

Women On The Move

Only when women have filled enough powerful positions will the pressure of moving up the corporate ladder be minimized. Women are facing more complicated questions than whether they belong in the top jobs. For many, the issue now is how far they will take their careers and whether they're getting the support they need.

During the 1980s women made strides in managerial and professional jobs, but still held less than 29 percent of all managerial jobs. In some areas of the country today, women now comprise more than half of all professionals, yet some blatant examples of discrimination still exist. Taking the step up will require that you are secure in your business savvy as well as yourself.

Women impatient with waiting for the top jobs are going into business for themselves. Businesses owned by women will dominate by the turn of the century, reported the National Association of Women Business Owners Foundation. One of the main reasons for women opening their own business is reflected in a broader and more human issue. A sizable number of the women striking out on their own are in their 40s and balancing being a professional, a homeowner, a parent and the child of aging parents.

The new attitude of a diversified workplace is good business sense which encourages the promotion of women. Today companies are thinking in light of matching the work force with the marketplace in which they do business. So with examples and a thrust toward promoting women, what are the stumbling blocks?

Stereotypes Still Exist

One of the reasons there aren't more women in key positions is the way women are stereotyped. The attributes that make women successful in other parts of their lives are not what business values and when confronted with a choice between hiring a woman or a man, most companies are still prejudiced into choosing the male. This happens time and time again, regardless of the qualifications of both.

Women who are fortunate enough to get their foot in the door and be hired are not able to put this prejudice behind them. Even today in office meetings, women are seeing the stunned shock when topics that were generally considered above their heads, is now their bailiwick.

So what do you do? You must be patient and understanding. It won't help to point out the prejudices, but it will help if you continue to demonstrate your professional attitude and capability to do the job. But you need to be able to recognize when a situation is getting out of hand. When will having the brains and portraying a business image be the only concern? Your guess is as good as mind.

Pay Gap

There's a $100,000 gap in the average salaries of male and female senior executives. This was reported in a UCLA's research finding. The study found an average salary of $187,000 a year for executive women in 1992 was offset by a $289,000 a year for male executives in 1989.

In Conclusion

The day has yet to come when men and women are treated on an equal footing. This should not discourage you to strive for success in business, but instead encourage you to meet the challenge. I know you are saying, "I've raised my children and paid my dues, so why should I have to put up with this?" I can only answer by saying that you take the time to look at both sides of the coin. Consider for a moment that you have to undergo a serious operation and your doctor is suggesting that you allow his son/daughter who is a recent graduate of medicine to perform the surgery. Unless you are a really unique person, you are not going to jump at the opportunity of being any doctor's first patient!

If success in the world of business is your goal, the lessons you have completed in this book will play an important role in your success. If you put it all together, not leaving anything to chance, you give yourself the best opportunity to achieve your goal.

www.ingramcontent.com/pod-product-compliance
Lightning Source LLC
Chambersburg PA
CBHW032119040426
42449CB00005B/196